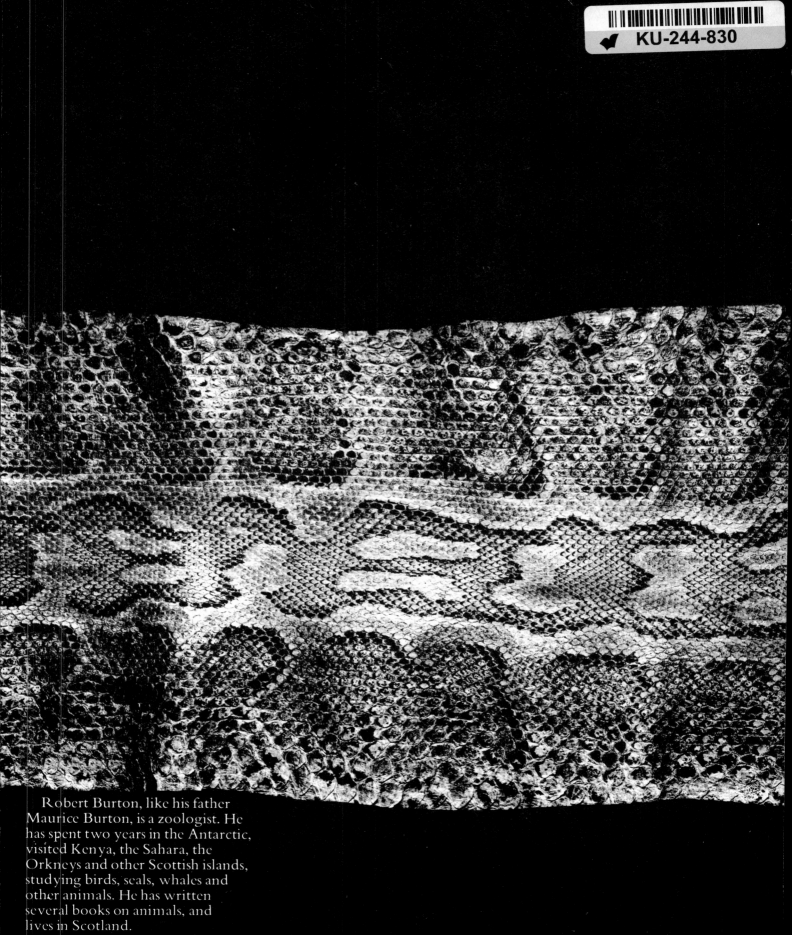

Robert Burton, like his father
Maurice Burton, is a zoologist. He
has spent two years in the Antarctic,
visited Kenya, the Sahara, the
Orkneys and other Scottish islands,
studying birds, seals, whales and
other animals. He has written
several books on animals, and
lives in Scotland.

First published 1974
Reprinted 1974
Macdonald and Co
(Publishers) Limited
St Giles House
49-50 Poland Street
London W1

Made and printed by
Morrison and Gibb Limited
Edinburgh, Scotland

Editor
Kate Woodhouse

Assistant Editor
Lesley Firth

Illustrators
Malcolm McGregor
Peter Connolly
Stephen Bennett
Pat Lenander

Production
Philip Hughes

Source of Photographs
National Gallery

ISBN 0 356 04504 8

The Life of

Reptiles
and Amphibians

A simple introduction to the way reptiles and amphibians live and behave. Special reference and projects section.

Macdonald
Educational

**Dr Maurice Burton
and Robert Burton**

The Life of Reptiles and Amphibians

Reptiles have a scaly skin and mostly live on land; amphibians can live on land, but must return to water to breed. There is a wide range of animals that make up these two groups. Snakes and crocodiles are both reptiles, frogs and newts are both amphibians.

There are many ways in which the behaviour of reptiles and amphibians varies. Crocodiles swim, snakes crawl, tortoises walk, a few lizards can fly; frogs jump, but newts swim or crawl.

Most amphibians are harmless, but did you know that there is a frog whose poison can kill a man? Some snakes are highly poisonous, like the coral snake. Did you know that there is a harmless snake called the milk snake that has the same markings as the coral snake which protect it from enemies? Did you know that a lizard will throw off its tail to escape from an enemy, and that it will then grow a new one?

These are just some of the exciting subjects covered in this book. There is a reference section at the end with even more information. The projects section tells you how to keep some reptiles and amphibians as pets, both indoors and outdoors.

Contents

Reptiles of the Past

Millions of years ago reptiles dominated the earth.

Triceratops, a horned dinosaur, was 6.2 m (20 ft) long. The hind part of its skull was carried backwards in a bony frill over the neck. It lived in what is now called the Gobi desert. Some of its eggs have been found fossilized there.

Proganochelys was one of the first tortoises. Its fossil remains are found in Germany. Its shell was 60 cm (2 ft) long. It looked very like the tortoises of today but it had small teeth and it could not draw its head into its shell.

Tyrannosaurus was the largest meat-eating dinosaur. It lived in North America. It was 14.3 m (47 ft) long and stood 4.6 m (15 ft) high. Its head was 1.2 m (4 ft) long and its jaws were armed with sharp teeth 10–12.5 cm (4–5 ins) long.

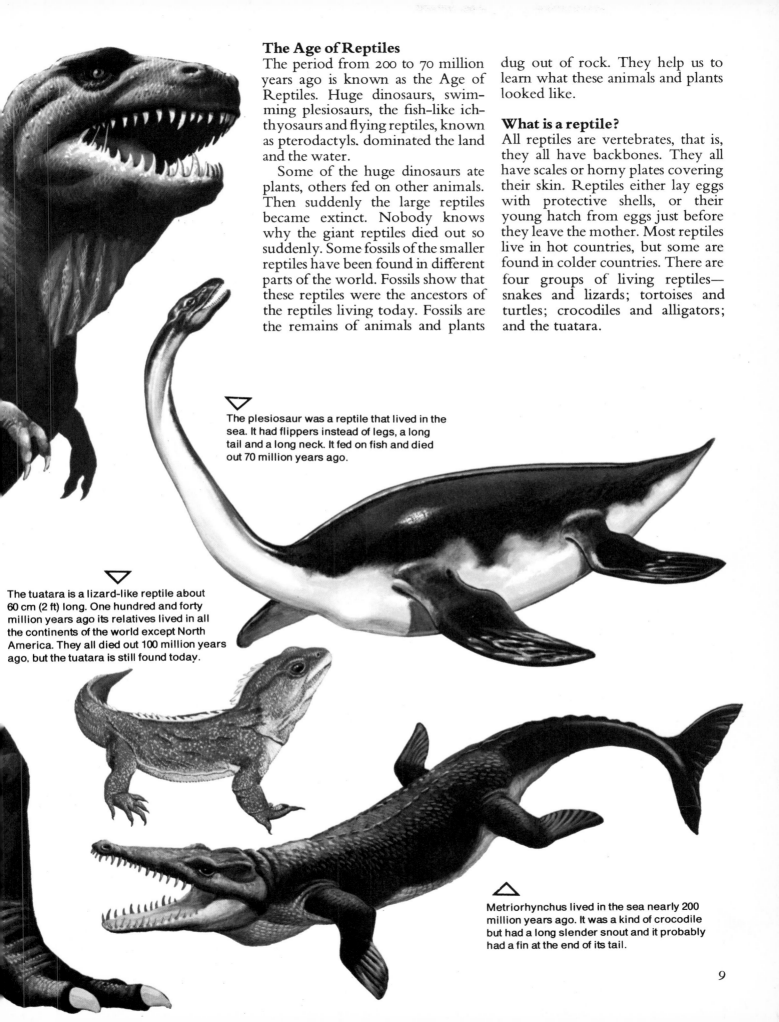

The Age of Reptiles

The period from 200 to 70 million years ago is known as the Age of Reptiles. Huge dinosaurs, swimming plesiosaurs, the fish-like ichthyosaurs and flying reptiles, known as pterodactyls. dominated the land and the water.

Some of the huge dinosaurs ate plants, others fed on other animals. Then suddenly the large reptiles became extinct. Nobody knows why the giant reptiles died out so suddenly. Some fossils of the smaller reptiles have been found in different parts of the world. Fossils show that these reptiles were the ancestors of the reptiles living today. Fossils are the remains of animals and plants dug out of rock. They help us to learn what these animals and plants looked like.

What is a reptile?

All reptiles are vertebrates, that is, they all have backbones. They all have scales or horny plates covering their skin. Reptiles either lay eggs with protective shells, or their young hatch from eggs just before they leave the mother. Most reptiles live in hot countries, but some are found in colder countries. There are four groups of living reptiles—snakes and lizards; tortoises and turtles; crocodiles and alligators; and the tuatara.

The plesiosaur was a reptile that lived in the sea. It had flippers instead of legs, a long tail and a long neck. It fed on fish and died out 70 million years ago.

The tuatara is a lizard-like reptile about 60 cm (2 ft) long. One hundred and forty million years ago its relatives lived in all the continents of the world except North America. They all died out 100 million years ago. but the tuatara is still found today.

Metriorhynchus lived in the sea nearly 200 million years ago. It was a kind of crocodile but had a long slender snout and it probably had a fin at the end of its tail.

9

A Living Fossil

The tuatara is one of the most ancient reptiles alive today.

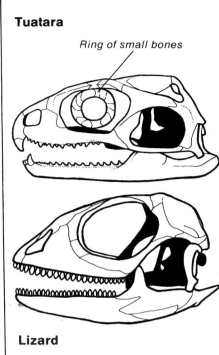

Tuatara

Ring of small bones

Lizard

The tuatara is not a true lizard although it looks very like one. The picture shows how the tuatara is different from a lizard. The teeth and skull bones are different and the tuatara cannot open its mouth as wide as a lizard can. It also has a ring of small bones round the eyeball which extinct reptiles had.

What is a living fossil?

The tuatara is the only survivor of a large group of ancient reptiles, called the Rhynchocephalia, that lived in the Age of Reptiles 200 to 70 million years ago. When the skull of one was sent to the British Museum in 1831 it was thought to belong to a new species of lizard. Thirty years later it was realized that it was just like the fossils that had been found of reptiles living millions of years ago. That is why it is called a living fossil. It has, in fact, changed very little in the last 140 million years.

The tuatara looks like a fairly large lizard 60 cm (2 ft) or more long. It lives off the mainland of New Zealand on rocky islands, which are shown in the red areas on the map. The name "tuatara" is Maori for "peaks on the back". The males in particular·have triangles of skin along the back.

A third eye

The tuatara is remarkable also for having the remains of an organ on the top of its brain. This has always been called the tuatara's third "eye". Nobody is sure what this "eye" was used for, or is used for today. It is possible that it heips to regulate the body temperature.

This reptile grows very slowly. One has been measured to grow by 15 mm (0.5 ins) in eight years.

A Living Dragon

The Komodo dragon is the largest lizard in the world.

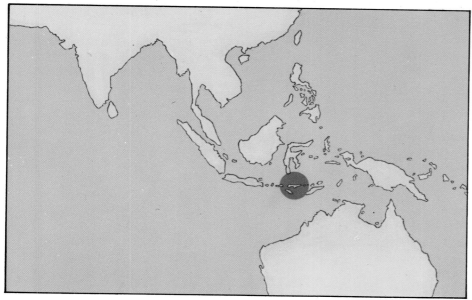

A giant lizard

The Komodo dragon grows up to 3 m (10 ft) long and weighs up to 140 kg (300 lb). It lives on a few small islands of Indonesia ringed on the map in red. The biggest of these islands is called Komodo. As nobody lived on Komodo very little was known about this giant lizard for a long time. The pearl fishers and turtle hunters who visited the island said they saw a crocodile about 6 m (19.5 ft) long.

The dragon is not as ferocious as these people thought, but it will sometimes kill and eat pigs, monkeys and even deer. After a big meal, a Komodo dragon will rest for a week without eating.

Armour Plating

Most turtles and tortoises have a bony shell to protect their body.

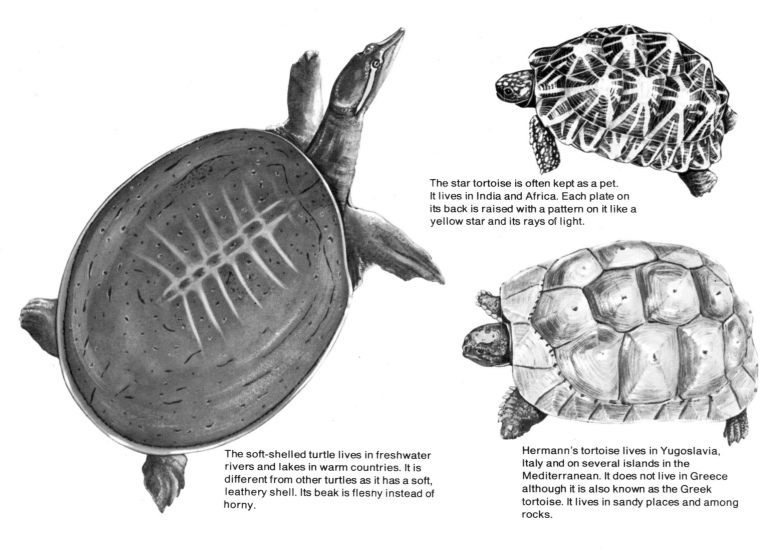

The star tortoise is often kept as a pet. It lives in India and Africa. Each plate on its back is raised with a pattern on it like a yellow star and its rays of light.

The soft-shelled turtle lives in freshwater rivers and lakes in warm countries. It is different from other turtles as it has a soft, leathery shell. Its beak is fleshy instead of horny.

Hermann's tortoise lives in Yugoslavia, Italy and on several islands in the Mediterranean. It does not live in Greece although it is also known as the Greek tortoise. It lives in sandy places and among rocks.

Inside a tortoise

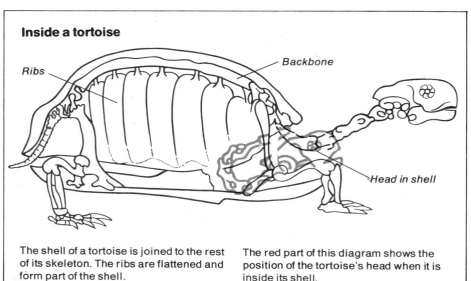

Ribs

Backbone

Head in shell

The shell of a tortoise is joined to the rest of its skeleton. The ribs are flattened and form part of the shell.

The red part of this diagram shows the position of the tortoise's head when it is inside its shell.

Reptiles with shells

Turtles, terrapins and tortoises are all related. They form one of the four groups of reptiles. Most turtles and terrapins live in freshwater in warm countries. There are some turtles that live in the sea. Most tortoises live on land. Some tortoises and turtles live to a great age. Some giant land tortoises will probably live up to 200 years. Even pet tortoises can live as long as people if they are well cared for.

Protective shell

Except for three families of turtle, this group of reptiles has bony shells. The shell is a bony case covered with a layer of horn.

One of the smallest of the freshwater turtles in the eastern part of North America is the musk turtle. It lives mainly on the bodies of small dead animals. Musk turtles have such a strong smell that they are called stinkpots.

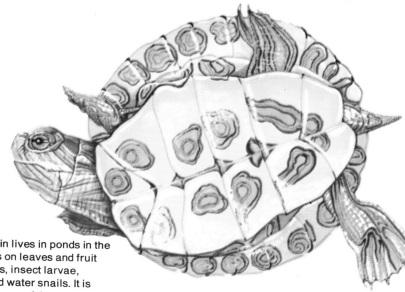

The red-eared terrapin lives in ponds in the United States. It feeds on leaves and fruit as well as small fishes, insect larvae, tadpoles, crayfish and water snails. It is called red-eared because of the patches of red on the sides of the head. These patches are not really ears.

The matamata of South America has an uneven shell with fringes of skin on its head and neck which small fishes and other animals mistake for weeds. As they swim towards it the matamata opens its mouth and the inrush of water carries the fishes in.

The snake-necked turtle of Australia is small. Its shell is not usually more than 12.5 cm (5 ins) long. This turtle cannot draw its long neck into its shell like other turtles. It bends its neck sideways along its shell instead.

Most tortoises and turtles are able to withdraw their legs and head into their shells when they are in danger. The shell is a very good protection against most enemies. A rat however may bite a tortoise and kill it even if it is drawn into its shell. A vulture, called a lammergeier or bearded vulture, will pick a tortoise up in its beak and drop it from a great height on to a stone to break its shell.

Hibernation

Tortoises that are brought to cold countries as pets rest during the winter to protect themselves against the cold. As soon as it is warm they move about and feed again.

Large numbers of Amazon river turtles gather on islands in the middle of the river each year to lay their eggs. The local Indians used to collect the eggs as soon as they were laid; 48 million were taken each year for food.

Journey to the Sea

Sea turtles will travel long distances to lay their eggs on special beaches.

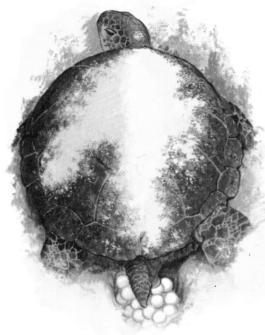

Laying the eggs

Sea turtles usually spend all their life in tropical seas, but the females must come on land to lay their eggs. They will travel many thousands of kilometres to lay their eggs. They come ashore at night and drag themselves up the beach. They dig a pit in the sand with their flippers. The pit is about 60 cm (2 ft) deep. The turtle lays a clutch of about 100 eggs in ten minutes in the hole and covers the eggs with sand. She lays about five clutches in one night. When it starts to get light she goes back to the sea.

Hatching

Some 7–10 weeks later the baby turtles hatch and fight their way to the surface. They usually come out at night when there is less danger from their enemies. Even at night the baby turtles know which way to go to the sea.

Very few baby turtles live to grow up. Dogs and people eat the eggs, and birds, crabs and snakes often eat the baby turtles. Turtles are not even safe in the sea.

Tropical seas

Nesting beaches

Inside and Outside

How a reptile is made up.

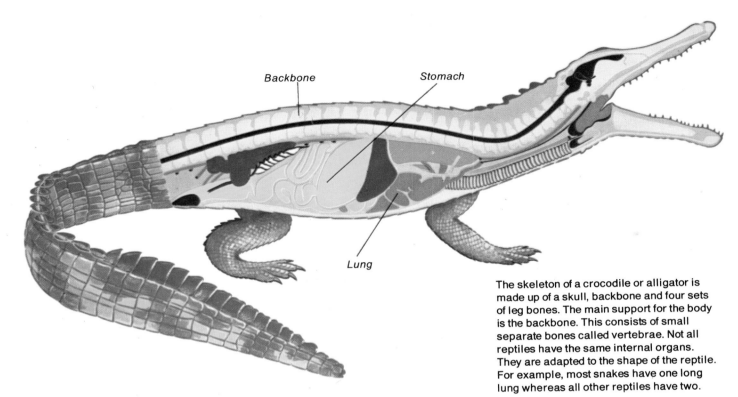

Backbone

Stomach

Lung

The skeleton of a crocodile or alligator is made up of a skull, backbone and four sets of leg bones. The main support for the body is the backbone. This consists of small separate bones called vertebrae. Not all reptiles have the same internal organs. They are adapted to the shape of the reptile. For example, most snakes have one long lung whereas all other reptiles have two.

Scales

The skin of reptiles has a cover of dry, tough scales. Except for three kinds of turtles, all reptiles have these scales. In tortoises and turtles and also crocodiles and alligators, the scales are strengthened by bony plates which form a heavy armour.

Snakes

The first reptiles had a fairly long body, a long tail and four short legs. Over many years one group of reptiles grew longer bodies and shorter legs. In the end they lost their legs altogether and became long and slender. These reptiles were the snakes. Snakes still have a tail, but it is difficult to see where the tail joins on to the body. Probably their shape changed as they took to burrowing.

Tortoises and turtles

Another group of reptiles became short and squat in the body. They were not very agile or quick in their movements. Instead of using speed to escape from their enemies they grew an armour of bone under the horny scales. This formed a kind of box to hold the internal organs. These reptiles are the tortoises and turtles.

Snakes have very long and flexible bodies, with a large number of vertebrae and ribs. A lizard may have 50 to 60 vertebrae and about 20 ribs. Snakes have 160 to 400 vertebrae and nearly the same numbers of pairs of ribs.

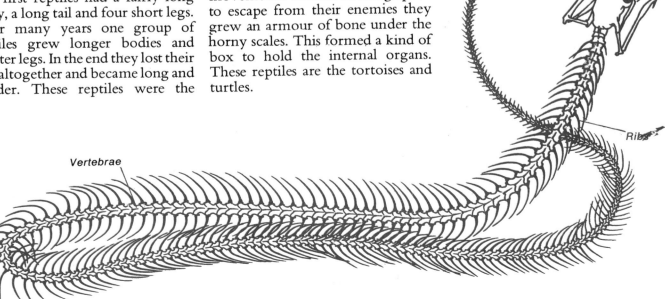

Ribs

Vertebrae

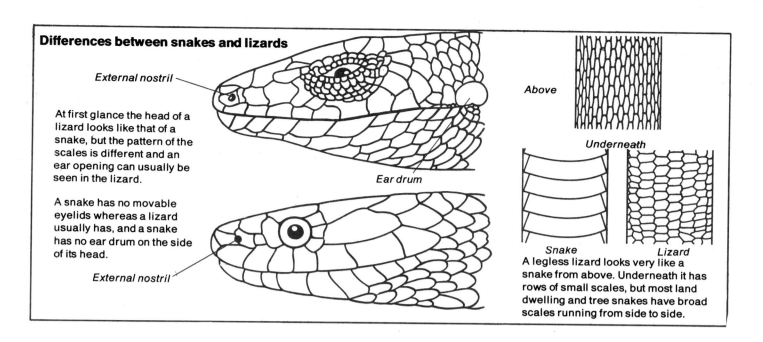

Differences between snakes and lizards

External nostril

At first glance the head of a lizard looks like that of a snake, but the pattern of the scales is different and an ear opening can usually be seen in the lizard.

A snake has no movable eyelids whereas a lizard usually has, and a snake has no ear drum on the side of its head.

External nostril

Ear drum

Above

Underneath

Snake   *Lizard*

A legless lizard looks very like a snake from above. Underneath it has rows of small scales, but most land dwelling and tree snakes have broad scales running from side to side.

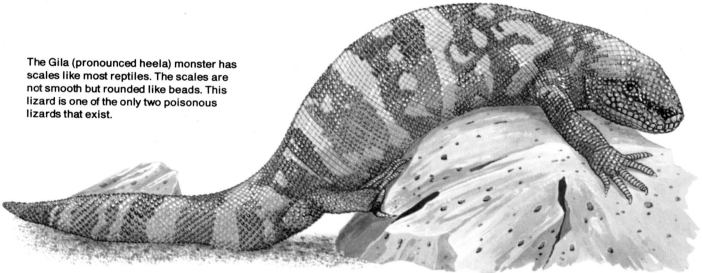

The Gila (pronounced heela) monster has scales like most reptiles. The scales are not smooth but rounded like beads. This lizard is one of the only two poisonous lizards that exist.

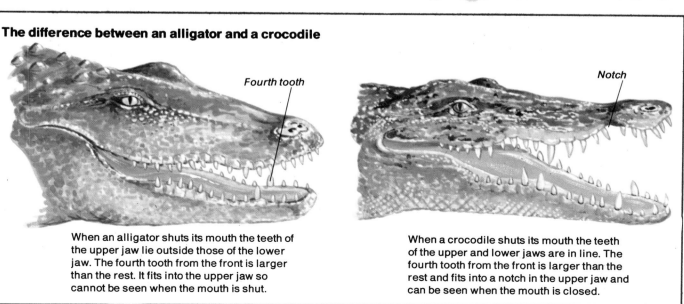

The difference between an alligator and a crocodile

Fourth tooth

Notch

When an alligator shuts its mouth the teeth of the upper jaw lie outside those of the lower jaw. The fourth tooth from the front is larger than the rest. It fits into the upper jaw so cannot be seen when the mouth is shut.

When a crocodile shuts its mouth the teeth of the upper and lower jaws are in line. The fourth tooth from the front is larger than the rest and fits into a notch in the upper jaw and can be seen when the mouth is closed.

Senses

The most important sense of reptiles is sight. Some reptiles have developed special sense organs.

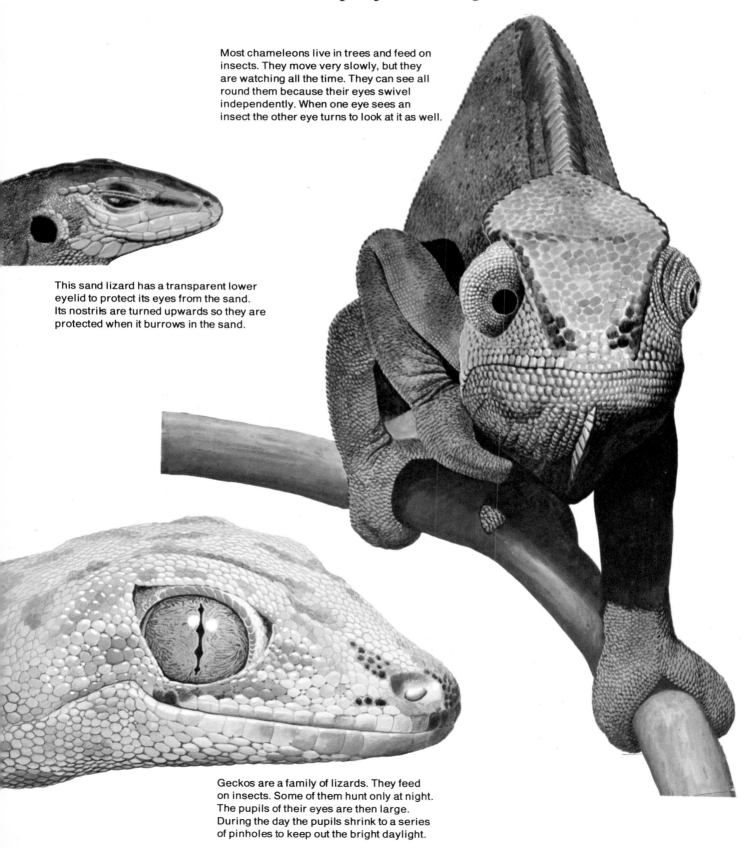

Most chameleons live in trees and feed on insects. They move very slowly, but they are watching all the time. They can see all round them because their eyes swivel independently. When one eye sees an insect the other eye turns to look at it as well.

This sand lizard has a transparent lower eyelid to protect its eyes from the sand. Its nostrils are turned upwards so they are protected when it burrows in the sand.

Geckos are a family of lizards. They feed on insects. Some of them hunt only at night. The pupils of their eyes are then large. During the day the pupils shrink to a series of pinholes to keep out the bright daylight.

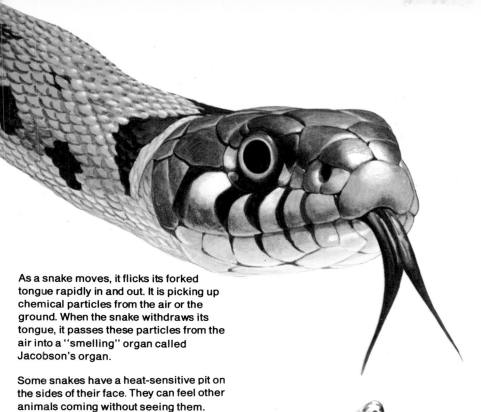

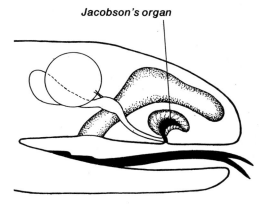

This diagram shows Jacobson's organ in the roof of the mouth of a snake. This organ is connected with the brain. It acts as a second organ of smell.

As a snake moves, it flicks its forked tongue rapidly in and out. It is picking up chemical particles from the air or the ground. When the snake withdraws its tongue, it passes these particles from the air into a "smelling" organ called Jacobson's organ.

Some snakes have a heat-sensitive pit on the sides of their face. They can feel other animals coming without seeing them.

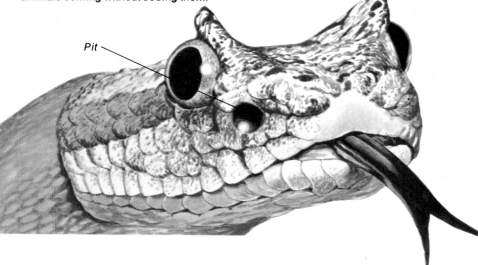

Binocular vision

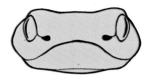

The eyes of most snakes are on the sides of their head so they see different things with each eye. Two kinds of tree-living snakes have narrow snouts so they can see things with two eyes and can judge distances well.

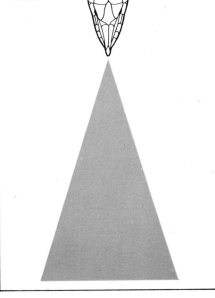

Sight
Most reptiles depend on their eyes for finding their food. Many animals can only see black, white and grey, but most reptiles can see colour. This helps them to see insects and other animals. Some reptiles react to colour in their courtship displays.

Eyelids
Reptiles' eyelids are very different from ours. Snakes look as if they do not have any eyelids—in fact their eyelids are immovable and the eyes are covered by a transparent window called a spectacle. Most lizards have movable eyelids. But in some kinds, particularly in those living in deserts, there is a small "window" in the lower lid. A few lizards have fixed lids and a spectacle like a snake's.

A special sense
Some reptiles do not have very good sight but have other senses to help them find food. Rattlesnakes and pit vipers have a pit each side of their head which can detect changes of heat. When an animal passes one of these snakes, the snake feels the heat of its body. It can detect a temperature change of less than 1°C. These snakes can catch food even if they are blindfolded.

Moving Along

Reptiles move along in every possible way. Some walk, some run, some swim, some crawl and some even fly.

When an alligator swims it brings its legs to the sides of its body. It drives itself through the water with side-to-side movements of its powerful tail. Most alligators and crocodiles do not swim for long distances.

The basilisk, a lizard of tropical America, has hind legs that are longer than its fore legs. It can run on its hind legs only. If it has to cross water it can run a few paces on top of the water.

In South-East Asia there is a flying lizard, or flying dragon. It has a web of skin on either side of the body, supported by long movable ribs. These can be opened and closed like fans. The lizard launches itself from a tree and glides up to 7 m (20 ft).

Walking on glass

Geckos can climb glass. They have sharp claws and scales on the soles of their feet covered with tiny bristles that grip the surface.

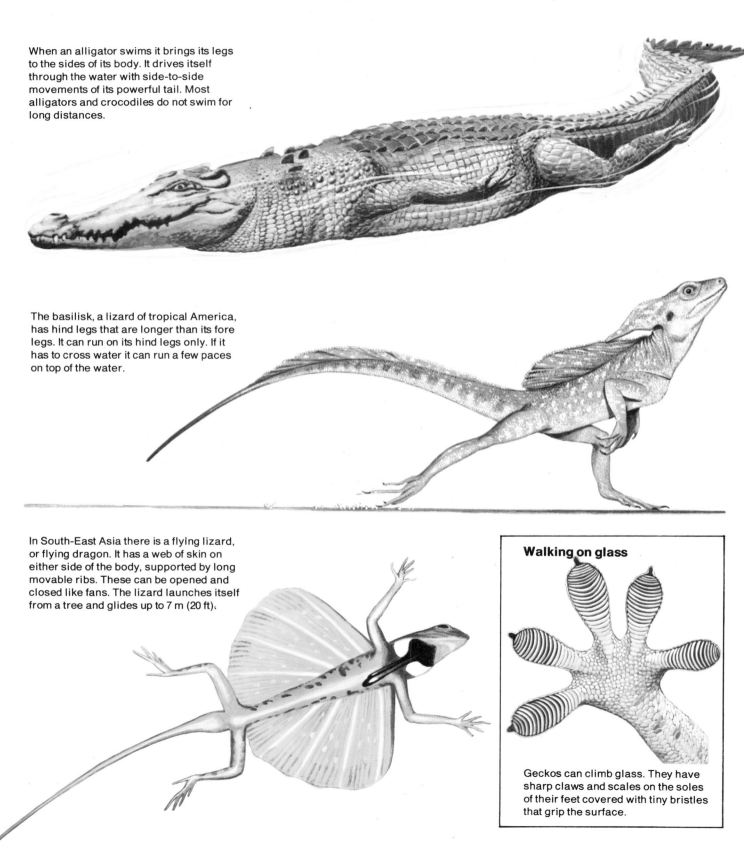

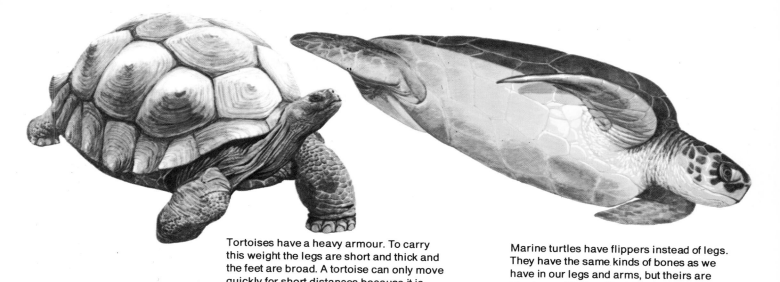

Tortoises have a heavy armour. To carry this weight the legs are short and thick and the feet are broad. A tortoise can only move quickly for short distances because it is so heavy.

Marine turtles have flippers instead of legs. They have the same kinds of bones as we have in our legs and arms, but theirs are shorter and flatter. Each flipper is used as a paddle for swimming.

Tortoises move slowly

Animals must move about to look for food, to find a mate and to escape from enemies. Some reptiles are able to move very fast and others can move only slowly. Tortoises, for example, do not move fast, mainly because they do not need to. Their shell protects them from many enemies and they eat mainly plant food.

The "high walk"

Crocodiles and alligators walk awkwardly though they swim very well. Sometimes they walk with the body lifted off the ground, doing what is called a "high walk". Usually they just crawl around with their body flat on the ground.

Quick escapers

Lizards move very fast. They have to be quick to escape their enemies and to catch food. They usually run very fast for short distances. Lizards are not often found far from some sort of shelter.

In the past

A hundred million years ago the giant reptiles were very slow. Some people think that many of them were killed because they could not escape from their smaller but quicker enemies. Dinosaurs were slow and heavy, but they did not make the ground shake as they walked, as is often said.

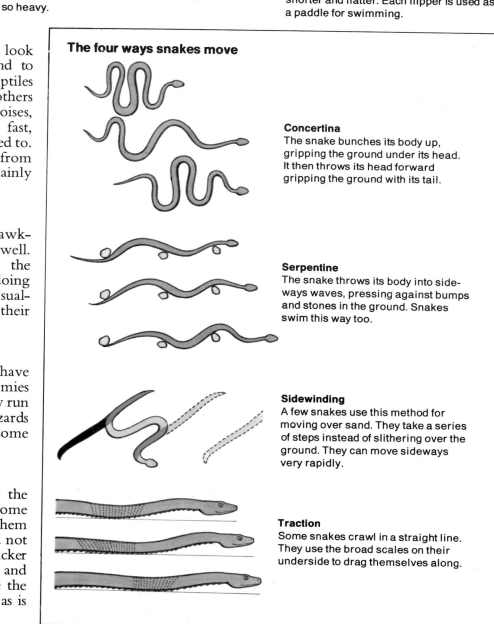

The four ways snakes move

Concertina
The snake bunches its body up, gripping the ground under its head. It then throws its head forward gripping the ground with its tail.

Serpentine
The snake throws its body into sideways waves, pressing against bumps and stones in the ground. Snakes swim this way too.

Sidewinding
A few snakes use this method for moving over sand. They take a series of steps instead of slithering over the ground. They can move sideways very rapidly.

Traction
Some snakes crawl in a straight line. They use the broad scales on their underside to drag themselves along.

Camouflage

Most animals have a natural means of keeping out of sight of their enemies. This is helped by their camouflage.

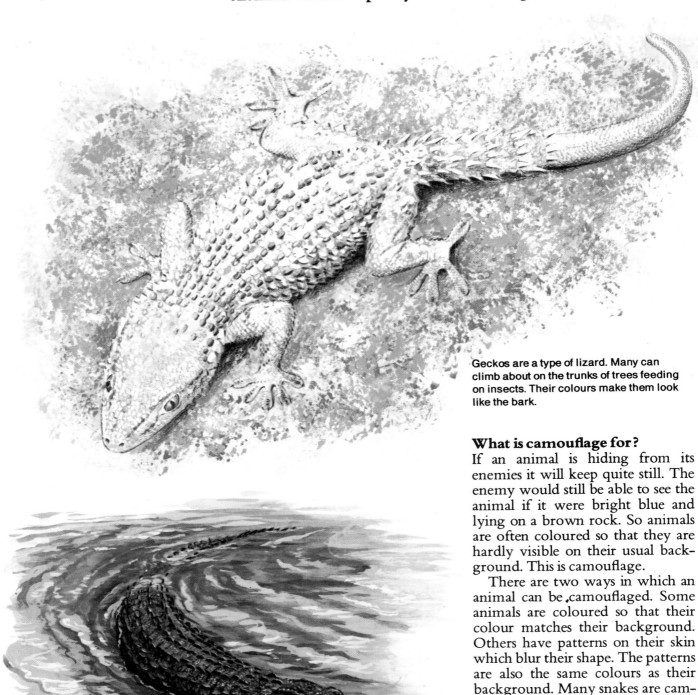

Geckos are a type of lizard. Many can climb about on the trunks of trees feeding on insects. Their colours make them look like the bark.

Alligators often live in muddy water, or water in which plants such as algae are growing. Their bodies are mud-coloured.

What is camouflage for?

If an animal is hiding from its enemies it will keep quite still. The enemy would still be able to see the animal if it were bright blue and lying on a brown rock. So animals are often coloured so that they are hardly visible on their usual background. This is camouflage.

There are two ways in which an animal can be camouflaged. Some animals are coloured so that their colour matches their background. Others have patterns on their skin which blur their shape. The patterns are also the same colours as their background. Many snakes are camouflaged in both these ways.

The chameleon

The chameleon has its own particular camouflage. When it is on a brown background it becomes a brownish colour. If it is on a green background it becomes greenish. However, it cannot change to tartan

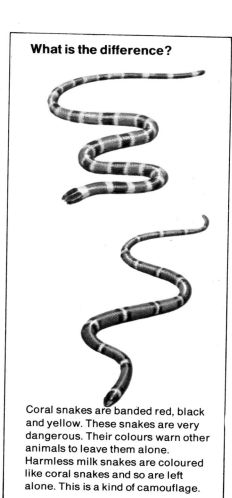

Coral snakes are banded red, black and yellow. These snakes are very dangerous. Their colours warn other animals to leave them alone. Harmless milk snakes are coloured like coral snakes and so are left alone. This is a kind of camouflage.

The Gaboon viper of West Africa is almost invisible when it is lying among dead leaves on the ground of a forest. It does not need to chase its prey because its prey walks up to it without noticing that it is there.

as some people think. It will only change to different browns and greens.

Enemies are camouflaged

Some enemies are also camouflaged. Sometimes the enemy will lie still and the prey will move nearer to it without being able to see it. For example, an animal drinking at the riverside may not see a crocodile waiting on the muddy bank.

The fishing snake lives in water. Water plants called algae grow on its back so it is camouflaged in water. It has two scaly tentacles on the tip of its snout. It is thought that these also act as lures. When the snake moves these they look like worms. Small fishes come to eat them and are caught by the snake.

The boomslang is an African snake that lives in trees. Its greenish colour hides it among the leaves so it can creep up on chameleons living in the trees.

23

A Second Skin

Snakes and lizards all shed their skin from time to time. This is called sloughing.

The outer horny layer of a reptile's skin is colourless and nearly transparent. When a chameleon is about to slough it seems to go white. Its skin peels off in many pieces.

How is it done?

All the time, we and some animals are shedding our skin in tiny flakes. These flakes are so small that they are hard to see. Crocodiles, tortoises and turtles also do this. Most lizards shed their skin in large flakes, but snakes usually shed their skin whole. When snakes and lizards shed their skin it is called sloughing (sluffing). It takes place several times a year.

During the slough only the outer horny layer of skin comes away. First it separates from the living skin underneath. Then it splits. A lizard may tug at it or rub against something hard to help it come off.

This sand lizard sheds its skin in one piece. After sloughing, the colours of the reptile are brighter. The animal looks as if it has been polished.

Milky eyes

When a reptile is about to slough, its eyes seem to go milky. This is because the dead skin is separated from the living skin underneath it.

Snakes shed their skin in one piece. The skin starts to peel off from the head. It turns inside out until all the skin is completely separate from the snake.

How a rattlesnake rattles

A new-born rattlesnake has a "button" on the end of its tail. The first time it sloughs, a piece of the dead skin is left covering the button. Each time the rattlesnake sloughs, another piece is left behind. These pieces of hard skin fit inside each other like a pile of thimbles. They are loose and rattle when the tail is waved.

Catching Food

Reptiles have many different ways of catching food.

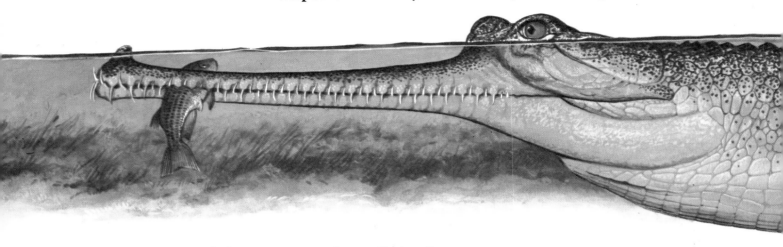

The gharial is a crocodile living in the rivers of India. It has a long, slender snout which it uses to snap up fish. It is not dangerous to humans, but it probably eats the flesh of animals drowned in the rivers.

The snapping turtle lives in the rivers of North America. It has jaws as strong as a steel trap. It eats any live or dead animal that it can swallow. It also eats a lot of plant food. A snapping turtle is unusual because it will hold food under a fore foot to tear it apart.

What do reptiles eat?

Most lizards feed on insects, spiders and snails but a few prefer plants. One lizard, the marine iguana of the Galapagos Islands, eats only seaweed.

Many lizards will eat eggs occasionally. The egg-eating snakes eat only eggs. Other snakes tend to feed on frogs, birds and small mammals. Young crocodiles feed almost entirely on insects. When they become fully grown they eat fish, other reptiles and mammals. Turtles and tortoises are mainly plant feeders but will also eat fish, frogs and dead animals.

Swallowing food whole

Most lizards, snakes and crocodiles swallow their food whole. They can get their food into their mouth in several ways. They can press the food against a solid object so it is pushed into the mouth. They can jerk their head back so that the food falls to the back of their mouth. Then they swallow it. Snakes have another method. The jaws of a snake are very flexible. They can move one jaw forwards and the other jaw backwards to draw food into the mouth.

Tortoises and turtles have no teeth. Their jaws are covered with very hard skin. The edge of this skin is sharp enough for cutting food.

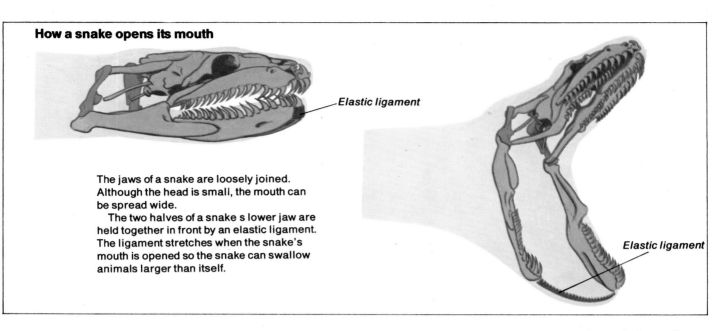

How a snake opens its mouth

Elastic ligament

The jaws of a snake are loosely joined.
Although the head is small, the mouth can
be spread wide.
   The two halves of a snake s lower jaw are
held together in front by an elastic ligament.
The ligament stretches when the snake's
mouth is opened so the snake can swallow
animals larger than itself.

Elastic ligament

The African egg-eating snake is usually
found near birds' nests. It wraps its jaws
round the egg and takes it into its mouth.
When the egg is in the gullet it is squeezed
against bones projecting from the
backbone. This cracks the shell. The snake
swallows the contents of the egg and spits
out the shell.

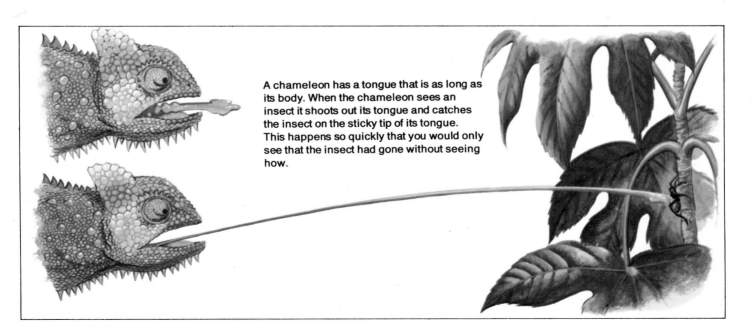

A chameleon has a tongue that is as long as
its body. When the chameleon sees an
insect it shoots out its tongue and catches
the insect on the sticky tip of its tongue.
This happens so quickly that you would only
see that the insect had gone without seeing
how.

Courtship and Breeding

Most reptiles lay eggs. In the others the eggs hatch just before being laid, so the young are born alive.

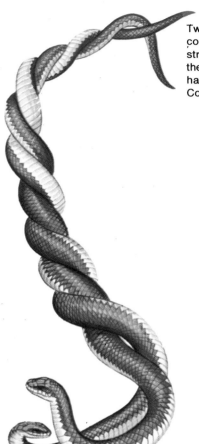

Two male snakes fighting over a territory coil their bodies round each other and struggle. It is a test of strength, and after it the weaker one goes away defeated. This has been called the "snake's dance". Contests like this are not often seen.

Male lizards, like the bearded lizard of Australia, open the mouth wide to show a coloured throat to display to a rival or a mate. The throat is either bright yellow, red or blue.

Courtship

Before reptiles mate there is usually a short courtship. In some species the male takes over a territory and defends it against other males. It is not always easy to tell whether two reptiles are courting or fighting. There is often the same display of colour in both.

A male tortoise courts the female by butting her and biting her legs. A snake rubs his chin along the female's back. Lizards display their colours to the females. At the same time they bob up and down using both their head and fore limbs to do this. Lizards also do this before fighting over territory.

Eggs

After mating, the females go away to lay their eggs. Reptiles usually lay their eggs in a hole in the ground so that they are hidden. Most eggs are white or yellow. The eggs do not have to be coloured for protection as they are usually buried. The eggs are round or oval.

The shell is usually soft and tough, like rubber, but some reptiles' eggs have chalky shells like birds' eggs. Sometimes the eggs are sticky when first laid and the whole clutch stick together until they hatch.

The eggs of a king cobra increase in size and weight before they hatch.

Most reptiles bury their eggs and leave them. Alligators and crocodiles make a nest. The female scrapes rotting plants together to cover the eggs, or pulls sand over them. Then she lies beside the nest or on it and drives away anything coming near it.

Birth from eggs

All reptiles are born from eggs. Usually the eggs hatch after the mother has laid them. Sometimes they hatch inside the mother before they are laid. This is called live birth.

Live birth

Some of the larger snakes, like this python, coil their body round their eggs. Most of the time the eggs are completely hidden. This protects the eggs from enemies and keeps them warm. When the eggs are ready to hatch the mother loosens the coils so that the young snakes can crawl out. The eggs have soft, leathery shells.

Sea snakes live in the Pacific and Indian Oceans. Most of them spend all their life at sea and give birth to living babies. The eggs form inside the mother's body, but they have very thin shells. The eggs hatch just as they are about to be laid and the baby snakes are born. Other sea snakes come ashore and lay eggs.

Baby snakes look like their mother except that they are much smaller. Even though the young snakes do not have to be taught how to catch food, they sometimes stay with their mother for several days before they wander away.

29

Means of Defence

Some reptiles have only feeble means of defence, or even none at all. Many reptiles use bluff.

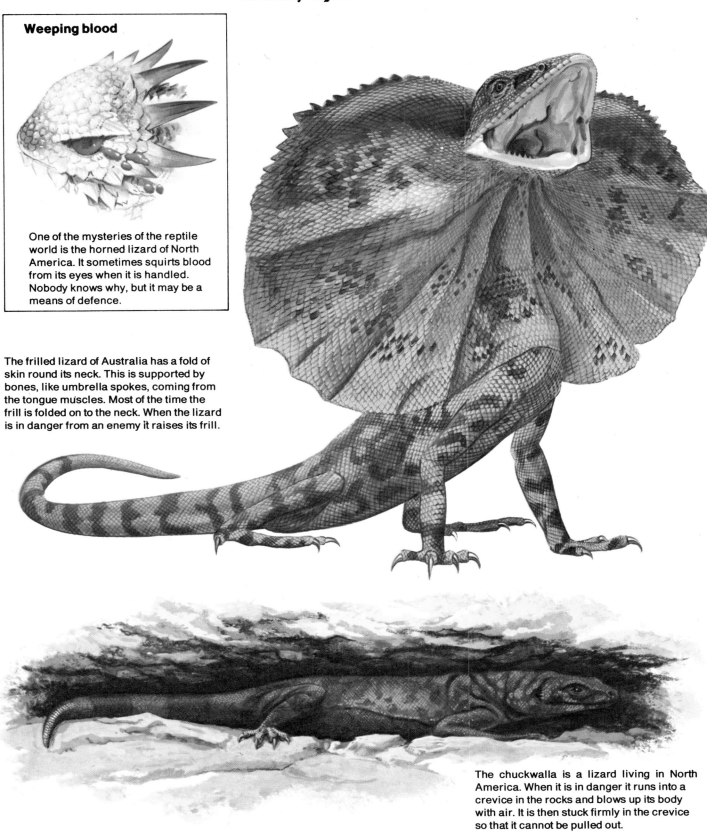

Weeping blood

One of the mysteries of the reptile world is the horned lizard of North America. It sometimes squirts blood from its eyes when it is handled. Nobody knows why, but it may be a means of defence.

The frilled lizard of Australia has a fold of skin round its neck. This is supported by bones, like umbrella spokes, coming from the tongue muscles. Most of the time the frill is folded on to the neck. When the lizard is in danger from an enemy it raises its frill.

The chuckwalla is a lizard living in North America. When it is in danger it runs into a crevice in the rocks and blows up its body with air. It is then stuck firmly in the crevice so that it cannot be pulled out.

Why is bluff important?

Many snakes and most lizards are not strong enough to defend themselves against their enemies. One means of defence they have is bluff. This means that they pretend to be something they are not. For example, they will pretend to be fierce when they are defenceless. This confuses their enemy who will probably then leave them alone. There are many different bluffs that these reptiles use.

No animal risks getting hurt if it can help it. Even an animal trying to kill for food must be careful its prey does not hit back. So every animal, no matter how big or ferocious, is on its guard in case it gets hurt. For example, the North American rattlesnake is deadly to many animals and some people say it uses its rattle to warn bigger animals not to tread on it.

Different bluffs

Some lizards change the colour of part of their body, usually the head and neck. Snakes hiss. Some lizards open their mouth wide to show a brightly coloured throat. Others blow themselves up so that they look larger than usual. All these are signals. They warn other animals not to touch them. Some lizards have a special breaking point in the tail. The lizard can throw off part of its tail. While its enemy watches this the lizard escapes. It then grows a new tail.

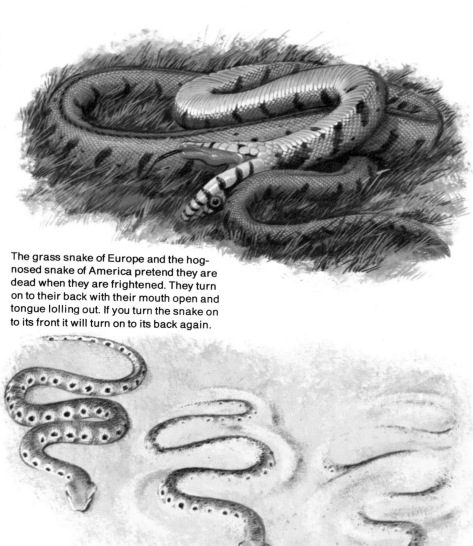

The grass snake of Europe and the hog-nosed snake of America pretend they are dead when they are frightened. They turn on to their back with their mouth open and tongue lolling out. If you turn the snake on to its front it will turn on to its back again.

This sand viper lives in deserts. It wriggles into the sand until only its eyes and nostrils are above the sand. It can see its enemies but its enemies cannot see it.

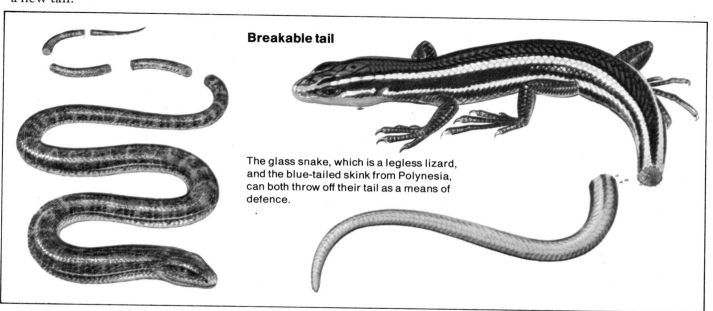

Breakable tail

The glass snake, which is a legless lizard, and the blue-tailed skink from Polynesia, can both throw off their tail as a means of defence.

Beware of Snakes

Some snakes are dangerous, others are harmless. It is hard to tell which is which. It is best to leave all of them alone.

Poisonous snakes

All snakes are dangerous to something, if only to the animals they eat. Not all snakes are dangerous to human beings. These snakes are called harmless because their poison is too weak to hurt people, and some, like boas, pythons and grass snakes, do not bite.

Snake poison is a kind of saliva from the venom glands. The snake's teeth are grooved or have a tube inside them. When the snake bites the venom flows down the teeth into the blood of the prey. The poison eventually kills the victim.

There are more poisonous snakes in Australia than in any other country.

The emerald tree boa of South America lives in trees and catches birds. Its colour disguises it in the leaves. When resting it balances its coils across a branch. When it strikes at a bird it can wrap its tail round the branch.

The anaconda kills its prey by wrapping its coils around the victim's body. The snake gradually tightens its coils so that its victim cannot breathe. It does not crush its victim.

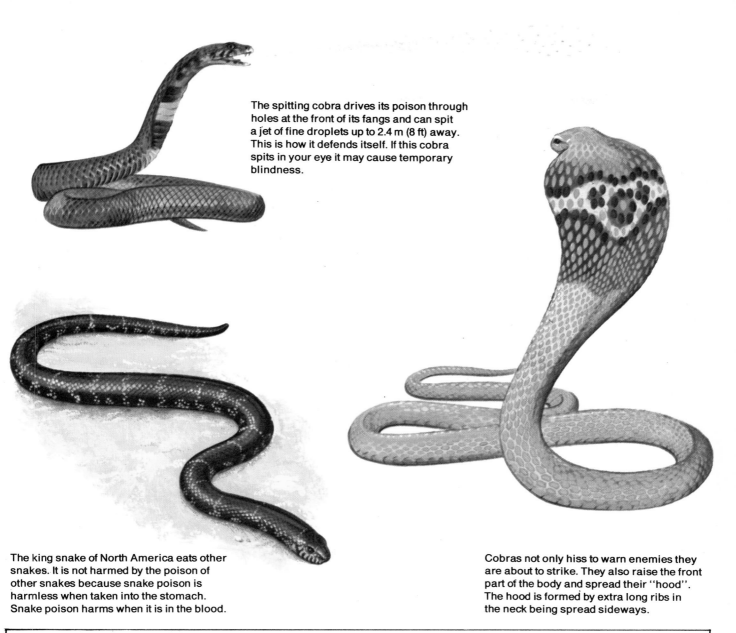

The spitting cobra drives its poison through holes at the front of its fangs and can spit a jet of fine droplets up to 2.4 m (8 ft) away. This is how it defends itself. If this cobra spits in your eye it may cause temporary blindness.

The king snake of North America eats other snakes. It is not harmed by the poison of other snakes because snake poison is harmless when taken into the stomach. Snake poison harms when it is in the blood.

Cobras not only hiss to warn enemies they are about to strike. They also raise the front part of the body and spread their "hood". The hood is formed by extra long ribs in the neck being spread sideways.

Different kinds of teeth

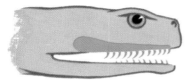

A few snakes, like the boas and pythons, are not poisonous. The teeth of poisonous snakes are of four types: teeth all alike, back fanged, front fanged and hinged front fanged. In the first the teeth are the same shape and size, and their poison is weak. In back-fanged snakes the venom flows along open grooves in small fangs which are far back in the upper jaw. The front-fanged snakes

have a pair of long grooved or tubular fangs that inject venom into the victim. In cobras, kraits and coral snakes, the fangs are rigid, but in vipers and rattlesnakes they are very long and fold back in the mouth when the jaws are closed. When these snakes open their mouths, the fangs swing down and forwards and stab the prey and at the same time the venom pours out.

Legends

Throughout history many legends have grown up about reptiles.

Thousands of years ago Egyptian kings wore head-dresses which were decorated with a model of a cobra. The cobra was thought to be a kind goddess who protected the king. The goddess was called Wadjyt, but she was also sometimes known as Buto.

The Aztecs who lived in Mexico made jewellery from many pieces of turquoise stone. This model of a snake, or serpent, was worn on the neck. It is about 10 cm (4 ins) wide. The Aztecs thought that the serpent was the most powerful of their gods.

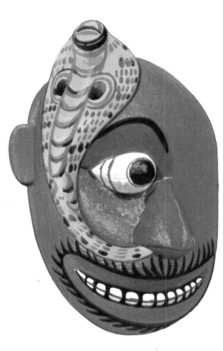

The people of Ceylon who made this mask thought that the snake had magical powers. The mask was worn by people who were deaf. The deaf person would wear the mask as part of a ceremony, which probably included a special dance, to cure their deafness.

The King of the Serpents

Serpents, or snakes as we call them today, have either been looked upon as dangerous animals bringing evil, or as very good ones bringing happiness.

In Europe in the Middle Ages, the most deadly animal was supposed to be the basilisk or cockatrice. It was called the King of the Serpents. According to legend, a basilisk was hatched from an egg laid by a cockerel in a dung-hill. The egg was guarded by a toad or snake until it hatched. The basilisk was like a cockerel, but it had a tail like a serpent's. It was so deadly that its look could kill.

An old story says that there was a knight who made himself a suit of mirrors. When he met a basilisk it looked at him and saw its own reflection in the mirror suit. The sight of its own reflection killed it. The city of Basle in Switzerland is said to be named after this basilisk.

How myths develop

Another story tells of an enormous snake seen in England in 1614. People said it was about 3 m (9 ft) long. The people who saw it wrote a description of it and from this we can be fairly sure it was only a large grass snake and therefore harmless. Even so, because they were very frightened by the snake they started to describe it as much more fierce than it really was. In the end it sounded as if they had seen a dragon. This is how myths develop.

Present-day myth

There is a legend about the European adder and the North American rattlesnake which some people still believe to be true. It says that the adder and rattlesnake's babies will glide into the mother's mouth when in danger. She swallows them and lets them out again when the danger has passed.

34

St George and the dragon

A dragon is a mythical monster, part serpent, part crocodile, with strong claws and scaly skin. It has wings and breathes out fire. The picture above was painted by Uccello, an Italian artist living during the 15th century. It shows St George killing a dragon, which was going to eat the young girl.

People in many countries, including China and Wales, have invented their own dragons. Dragons became popular in mythology as fierce animals that guarded treasure or held people prisoner. It was the task of heroes and knights to find a dragon and kill it in the same way as St George did.

The Soay monster

Soay is an island off the west coast of Scotland. Nearly a hundred years ago a man said he had seen a monster swimming in the sea around the island. A few years later another man saw it again. He told an artist what he had seen and the artist drew the top picture. However, a Dutch scientist says it was only a leathery turtle (lower picture).

Reptiles and Man

Many reptiles have been very badly treated by man. Some have been used to help man.

Charles Darwin, who lived in the 19th century, was one of the first people to talk about the evolution of modern animals, including man, from ancient species. The giant tortoise next to him is found on the Galapagos Islands. It was here that Darwin noticed that the birds and reptiles on each of the islands were different. He decided that this was caused by adaptation to the different conditions on each island. When animals adapt like this over a long number of years, we call this evolution—or "the survival of the fittest".

Years ago chemists' shops, or pharmacies, often had a stuffed crocodile or a stuffed tortoise hanging from the ceiling. Some of these old pharmacies had lots of other curious stuffed animals hanging from the ceiling or decorating the windows. Reptiles have often been used as medicines. One remedy from the 16th century was to take the skin of a crocodile, dry it and powder it and mix it with vinegar or oil. People believed that if this was placed on the body of a person who had to have an operation he would feel no pain.

The modern remedy for snake bite is for a doctor to inject what is called anti-venine into the victim. To get the anti-venine a snake is "milked". That is, somebody holds a snake behind the head and makes it bite on the edge of a glass or tumbler so that as the venom is given out it flows into the glass. It can then be used to make an anti-venine.

Reptiles for food and clothing

Man does not make as much use of reptiles as he does of other animals. Reptiles have been used mainly for food or for their skins. Some tribes in tropical countries eat the flesh of lizards and snakes. Snake flesh is considered a delicacy in Japan and North America. Crocodile and snake skin is used to make bags and shoes.

For centuries marine turtles have been killed for their flesh and in order to make turtle soup. Their eggs are eaten as well.

The killing of so many crocodiles for their skin and flesh has meant that some species may soon die out,

An interesting sight in India is the snake charmer. He goes around with a large basket containing a cobra. When a crowd gathers round him he takes out his musical pipe, lifts the lid off the basket and starts to play a tune. The cobra rears itself and spreads its hood and appears to be dancing to the music. Since snakes are deaf, the swaying has nothing to do with the sounds of the pipe but seems to be in imitation of the movements of the piper who sways from side to side as he plays.

unless they are protected by international laws against hunters.

Help from reptiles

Reptiles have been useful to man in other ways. Chameleons feed on disease-carrying insects such as flies. The same is true of geckos, lizards that come into houses in warm countries and run upside-down over the ceilings to catch insects. Many snakes feed on rats and mice and in some hot countries they are the main killers of these pests. Other ways in which reptiles are used, or ways in which they help man are shown on this page.

The Indian python is the most popular snake for snake dancing but sometimes other big snakes are used. Snakes should not be picked up or touched just before or after they have eaten. They should also be left alone when they are sloughing. They will be dangerous if disturbed.

37

What is an Amphibian?

Amphibian means leading a double life. Most amphibians live on land but breed in water.

Eustenopteron was a fish that lived in fresh water over 300 million years ago. It had two pairs of fins that were the beginnings of legs and it breathed with both gills and lungs.

Ichthyostega is the oldest known salamander. It lived over 300 million years ago. It had legs like the salamanders living today, but its tail fin had fin rays like a fish.

Seymouria is a fossil found in the United States. It was mainly like an amphibian, but also partly like a reptile. Fossil tadpoles of some of its relatives have been found.

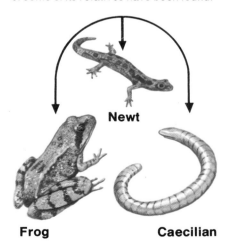

Newt

Frog   **Caecilian**

Three kinds of amphibians are living today. Newts and salamanders have long tails. Frogs and toads have tails when they are tadpoles but lose them when they grow up. Caecilians have no legs, are worm-like, and some have tiny scales in their skin.

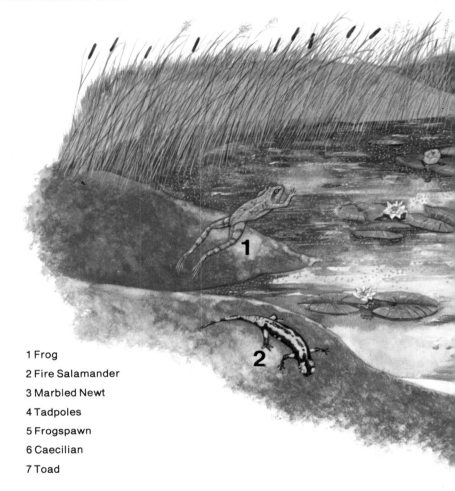

1 Frog

2 Fire Salamander

3 Marbled Newt

4 Tadpoles

5 Frogspawn

6 Caecilian

7 Toad

From fish to amphibian

Amphibians are descendants of some kinds of fishes. Some people think that millions of years ago many of the lakes in the world started to dry up. This meant that the fishes in these lakes had to change so they could live on the land. The fishes developed lungs, so they could breathe out of the water. They developed legs so they could walk on land. These were the first amphibians. When animals change like this, it is called evolution.

Different amphibians

This scene shows some of the kinds of amphibians living today. You would not find these amphibians together in one pond as they are here. Most amphibians live in a hot, wet climate. Frogs and toads belong to one order. Frogs have moist, smooth skin, but toads have dry, warty skin. Frogs are usually more aquatic than toads. Newts and salamanders belong to another order. Caecilians are a third order.

Eggs

Most amphibians lay their eggs in water. Amphibians' eggs do not have shells. If the eggs were laid on the ground, they would dry up before they were hatched. A baby frog, toad or newt is called a tadpole. Tadpoles are like fishes in several ways. They live in water and they breathe through gills.

Caecilians

Caecilians are amphibians living in warm countries. They have long bodies with no legs and look like earthworms. They are between 1.3 m (4½ ft) and 15 cm (6 ins) long. They are usually blind and live underground. Their eyes are often covered with skin. Many species have small scales buried in their smooth skin. These are the only amphibians with scales. Like other amphibians, they lay their eggs in water or in damp ground.

Breeding Time

Most amphibians must go to water to breed.

This reed frog has filled its throat pouch with air. To croak, it passes the air backwards and forwards across the vocal chords.

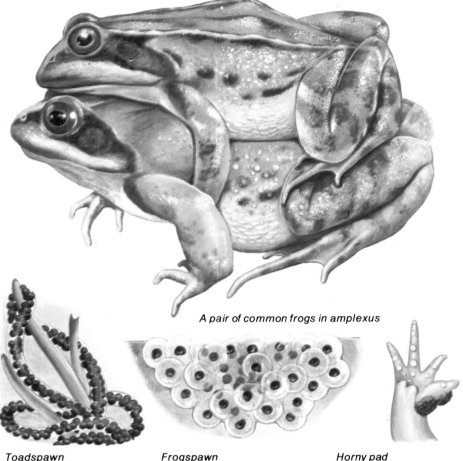

A pair of common frogs in amplexus

The male edible frog of Europe has a pair of vocal sacs, one either side of its mouth. These are used for croaking. The frog blows them up like small balloons.

Toadspawn *Frogspawn*

Toadspawn is in long strings with the eggs in rows. Toadspawn does not float. The jelly-covered eggs of frogs float at the surface of ponds.

Horny pad

During the breeding season some male frogs and toads have a pad of hard, rough skin at the base of their inner finger. They grip the female frog with this finger.

Ear

Frogs must be able to hear the croaks that the males make. The ear drum is a small round patch of light-coloured skin behind the eye.

Journey to the ponds

Frogs travel by huge leaps to the same ponds every spring to breed. Toads follow a few weeks later. Toads travel mostly at night in a long procession, always along the same route.

Amplexus

Usually the male frogs reach the pond first. When they are in the water they start to croak. As soon as a female reaches the pond several males swim towards her. One climbs on her back and clasps her under the armpits. This is called being in amplexus.

The female frog then begins to lay eggs. As she does so the male fertilizes them with his sperm. Each egg is surrounded by jelly. A mass of jelly-covered eggs is called the spawn.

Toads mate in deeper water than frogs. Toads' eggs are laid and fertilized in the same way as frogs' eggs. Toadspawn is in long strings instead of a mass. Toadspawn is often wound round water plants.

Back to land

A female frog or toad gives a special grunt when she has finished laying her eggs. The male leaves her and she goes back on land. The males return to land later.

Some tree frogs beat their spawn into a foam with their hind legs. The foam clings to leaves overhanging water. When the tadpoles are ready to go into the water the foam melts.

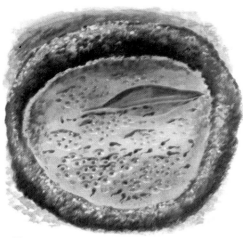

The smith frog makes a mud nest in shallow water for its eggs. It makes a circular wall of mud so it has a pond within a pond. When the tadpoles hatch they swim out into the main pond.

A male newt courts a female by beating water at her with his tail.

The male newt drops his sperm in small packets, called capsules, for the female to pick up with her cloaca.

The female marsupial frog has a pouch on her back to carry her eggs. The young leave the pouch as tadpoles or froglets. These frogs do not have to mate in water because their eggs are protected in the female's pouch.

The male midwife toad pushes his legs through the strings of eggs when they are laid. He carries them about with him and takes care of them. When they are ready to hatch he goes to a pond and the tadpoles swim away.

The female newt lays her eggs one at a time, each on a leaf. She folds the leaf round each egg with her hind feet.

A newt's egg on a leaf. It is sticky so it will not fall off.

The newt tadpole breathes with gills and has two legs.

The tadpole then develops another pair of legs. The gills will soon disappear and the tail will grow thicker.

The Stephen Island frog lays its eggs on land, on damp earth. The tadpoles do not hatch from the eggs as they could not survive on land. They hatch when they have changed to froglets.

The male Darwin's frog has long vocal sacs reaching back from his throat. He takes the eggs into the sacs. The young do not leave until they are froglets.

Growing Up

An amphibian changes in many ways between egg and adult.

Frogspawn is made up of many eggs, each in its own coat of jelly. Within this jelly the egg grows into an embryo. The jelly protects the embryo from the cold.

A few days after the embryo hatches it becomes a tadpole. It swims like a fish and it breathes through external gills. These are three feathery gills either side of the head. It starts to develop a mouth and to eat plant food.

Soon a fold of skin grows over the external gills and the tadpole now breathes through internal gills.

The fore legs start to grow first but are hidden under the skin over the gills. Then a pair of hind legs start to grow out at the base of the tail. The tadpole stops eating plant food and starts eating animal food.

As the hind legs grow longer, a pair of front legs burst out through the skin covering the gills. At the same time the tail begins to get shorter.

Finally the tadpole turns into a froglet with four legs and no tail. It can then come on land to live. It has grown a pair of lungs and can breathe with these.

The axolotl is a very unusual salamander. Axolotls are usually black or dark brown, but albinos like this one are quite common. Salamanders have feathery gills when they are young, but lose them before they are adult. The axolotl keeps its gills all its life, but it can breed like an adult. This is because it does not have a chemical called thyroxin in its glands. The water it lives in does not have this chemical in it. If an axolotl is given thyroxin it will become a fully-developed Mexican salamander.

Feeding

Amphibians can catch food with their teeth or with their tongue.

The tongue of a frog or toad is flat and broad. When a frog or toad sees an insect it opens its mouth and throws out its tongue.

The tongue moves so quickly that it whips the insect into the mouth. This movement takes less than one-tenth of a second.

When it is fully stretched, the tongue is nearly a third of the length of the frog or toad.

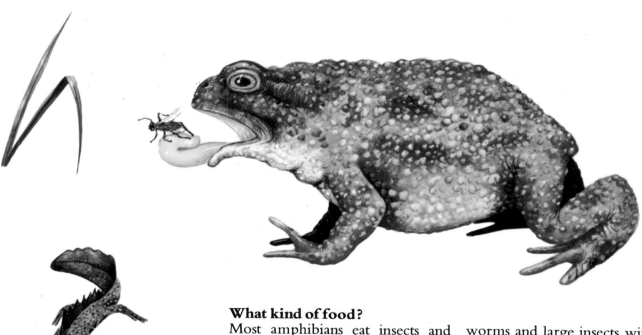

A newt or salamander usually snaps its food up with its jaws, especially when it is feeding underwater. Newts and salamanders eat worms, slugs, snails and insects.

What kind of food?

Most amphibians eat insects and other small animals, such as snails, slugs and worms. The larger the amphibian the larger the animals it can catch. Some of the very large frogs and toads catch and eat mice. When a tadpole hatches it will eat plant food. A few days later, it starts to feed on the bodies of small, dead animals in the water.

Catching food

Newts and salamanders usually catch their food by snapping it up with their jaws. They will sometimes use their tongue, although it is not very long. Frogs and toads mainly use their tongue, but seize worms and large insects with their jaws.

When the insect is in the mouth of a frog or a toad, it is crushed between the tongue and the eyeballs. The frog or toad looks as if it is closing its eyes tight when it swallows. This is because it is drawing its eyeballs down to crush the insect.

Finding food

Newts and salamanders find their food mainly by smell, whether they are on land or in water. Frogs and toads find theirs mainly by sight. They do not notice their food until it moves.

Enemies and Defence

Most amphibians have some way of protecting themselves. Even so they have many enemies.

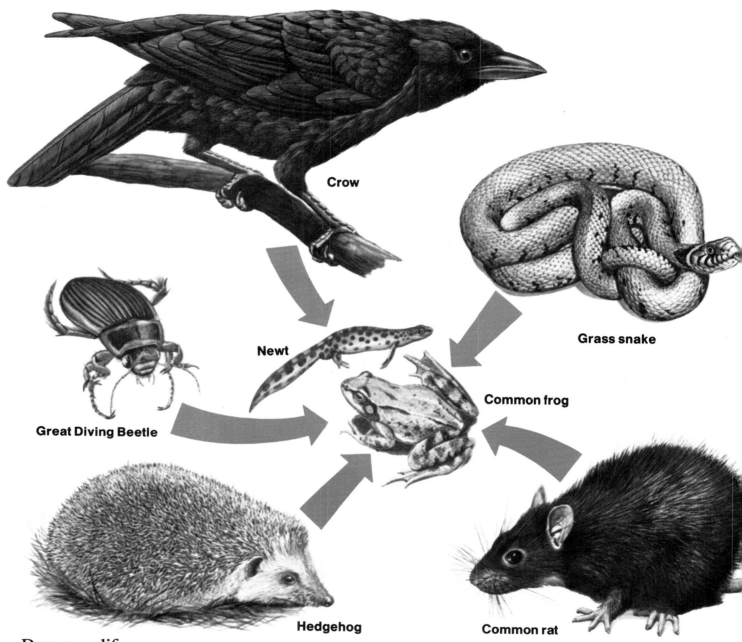

Crow

Grass snake

Newt

Great Diving Beetle

Common frog

Hedgehog

Common rat

Dangerous life
Amphibians are threatened by enemies all their lives, even before they are hatched from the spawn. Large quantities of spawn are taken every year for studying by school children. Most amphibians lay large numbers of eggs but very few of the young live to grow up. Certain insects, snakes, birds, rats and hedgehogs will all attack different amphibians and their eggs. Sometimes a large, old frog will even eat a small one.

Protection
The danger from enemies would be much greater if amphibians did not have some protection. Most of them are coloured or patterned so that it is difficult for their enemies to see them against their natural background. There are amphibians that only travel at night because this is the safest time for them. Frogs can jump to escape from some of their enemies.

Poison
Most amphibians have a certain amount of poison in their skin. Even so, this does not stop some of their enemies from eating them. Some amphibians are very brightly coloured, and these always have more poison in their skin.

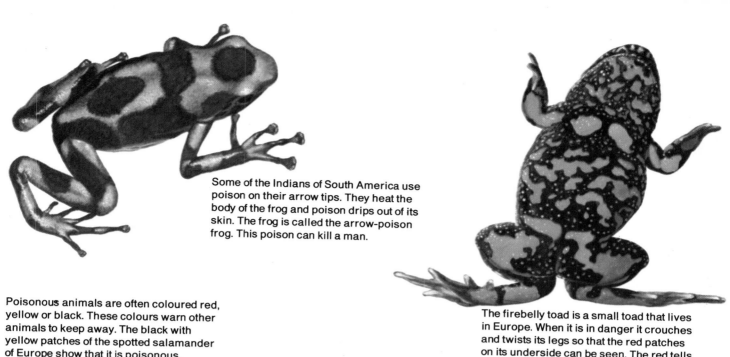

Some of the Indians of South America use poison on their arrow tips. They heat the body of the frog and poison drips out of its skin. The frog is called the arrow-poison frog. This poison can kill a man.

Poisonous animals are often coloured red, yellow or black. These colours warn other animals to keep away. The black with yellow patches of the spotted salamander of Europe show that it is poisonous.

The firebelly toad is a small toad that lives in Europe. When it is in danger it crouches and twists its legs so that the red patches on its underside can be seen. The red tells an enemy that the toad is very poisonous.

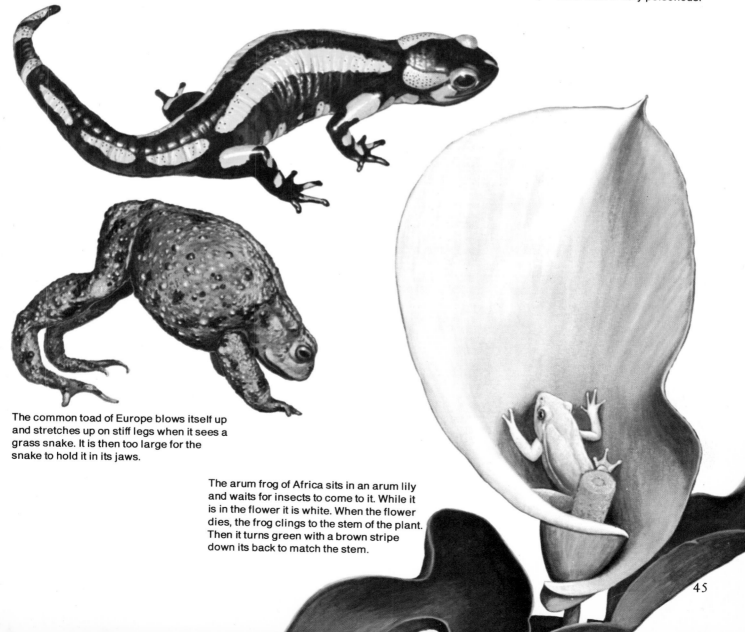

The common toad of Europe blows itself up and stretches up on stiff legs when it sees a grass snake. It is then too large for the snake to hold it in its jaws.

The arum frog of Africa sits in an arum lily and waits for insects to come to it. While it is in the flower it is white. When the flower dies, the frog clings to the stem of the plant. Then it turns green with a brown stripe down its back to match the stem.

On Land and in Water

Frogs jump, toads walk and newts crawl on land. They are all good swimmers.

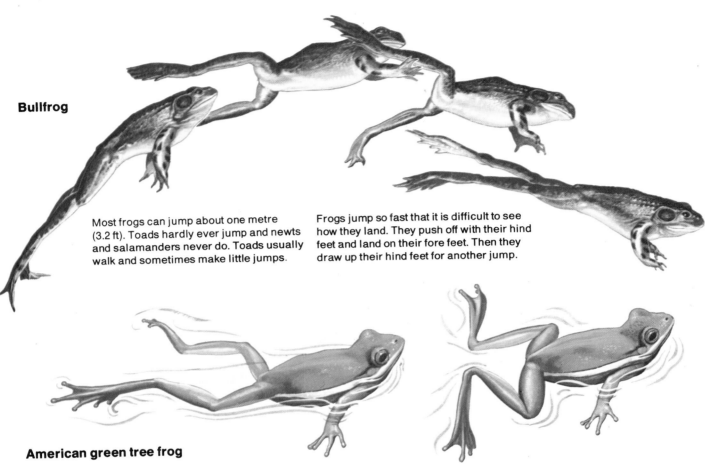

Bullfrog

Most frogs can jump about one metre (3.2 ft). Toads hardly ever jump and newts and salamanders never do. Toads usually walk and sometimes make little jumps.

Frogs jump so fast that it is difficult to see how they land. They push off with their hind feet and land on their fore feet. Then they draw up their hind feet for another jump.

American green tree frog

A tadpole swims rather like a fish, with side-to-side movements of its tail, but it

does not move its body. Frogs and toads swim in breast-stroke style. Sometimes

they use all four legs but more often they use only the hind legs.

Alpine newt

Marbled newt

A newt walks by moving a fore leg and the hind leg on the opposite side together. It can only move in a slow waddle.

A newt uses its body and its tail for swimming. When it is swimming, it holds its four legs against the sides of its body to

make a smooth shape for moving through the water. It can walk across the bottom of a pond as easily as it can walk on land.

Slowing Down

Amphibians rest during the winter.

In autumn frogs and toads look for a comfortable place to spend the winter. Usually frogs bury themselves about 3 cm (1¼ ins) below the surface of the mud at the bottom of a pond. They may rest on top of the mud or they may bury themselves under the damp grass near a pond. Toads often dig themselves deep into a dry bank. Sometimes they are found in the cellars of houses.

Only resting

In countries where winter is cold, amphibians of all kinds rest during the autumn and most of the winter. It is very difficult for them to find food in winter. They do not hibernate as some animals do. Hibernation means going to sleep for the winter.

If you throw a pebble into a pond where a frog is resting in winter, it will swim slowly away. If there is a warm day in the middle of winter frogs and toads might come out to look for food.

Underwater breathing

In winter, frogs and toads can stay under water for weeks or months on end. This is because they breathe more through their skin than through the mouth. They absorb oxygen for breathing through tiny blood vessels in the skin. They use very little oxygen because they are so still and their hearts beat very slowly. They do not need to eat as they use very little energy while they are resting.

Time to come out

Nobody knows how a frog can tell when it is time to leave its winter home. Somehow the frog knows when it is warm enough to come out and make its way to a pond to breed. Frogs seldom come out until the last ice is off the ponds.

Newts and salamanders living in cold countries often stay under stones for the winter.

Special Features

Some amphibians have special features.

Tree frogs live in warm countries in trees and shrubs. Each of their toes has a sucker at the tip. Tree frogs cling to the bark with these suckers. They can even climb up glass with them.

Adaptations

Some amphibians have special features which help them to live in different places. This is known as adaptation. The Surinam toad of South America lives in the water all the time. Its body is very flat. On each toe of its front feet it has what looks like tentacles. These tentacles help it to feel for food in the dark, muddy water where it cannot see.

Paradoxical frog

There are some amphibians with features that no one can explain, for example, the paradoxical frog of South America. A paradox is something that looks absurd and yet is true. The tadpole of this frog is about 250 mm (9.8 ins) long when fully grown, but the froglet is only about 38 mm (1.5 ins) long. The fully grown frog measures up to 75 mm (2.9 ins).

The male hairy frog looks as if it has patches of hair on its hind legs and sides. In fact these are a form of gills. This frog has very small lungs. In the breeding season the male is more active than the female and so needs more oxygen.

Frogs living in deserts in Australia fill their bladders very full when it rains. Then they burrow in the sand and stay there until it rains again. When the aborigines are thirsty they try to find a frog and dig it out of the sand. They squeeze it to get a drink. These frogs are called water-holding frogs.

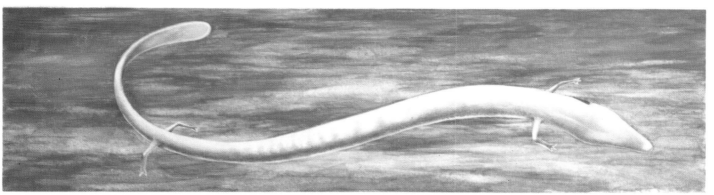

The olm is a strange salamander that lives in the underground rivers and pools of South-East Europe. It is white with a flush of pink, has bright red gills and is blind. The olm feeds on tiny shrimps and small fishes. When a young olm hatches it is almost black and has well-developed eyes. As it grows it becomes white and its eyes become useless.

Facts and Figures

REPTILES

Earliest known
The oldest known reptiles lived in Nova Scotia, in Canada, 290 million years ago.

Largest reptile
The largest reptile living today is the estuarine or salt-water crocodile which is usually 3.6–4.2 m (12–14 ft) long. The greatest recorded length was 8 m (27 ft), for one killed in the Philippines in 1823. Its weight was said to be about two tons.

Smallest reptile
A tiny gecko found on only one of the Virgin Islands in the West Indies measures under 18 mm (0.71 ins) long with a tail of about the same length.

Largest lizard
The Komodo dragon usually grows to 3 m (10 ft) long and up to 140 kg (317 lbs) weight. The largest ever recorded was 3 m (10 ft 2 ins) long and weighed 164 kg (365 lbs).

Largest turtle
The leatherback turtle measures up to 2.1 m (7 ft) long and 2.1 m across the front flippers. It weighs up to 360 kg (800 lbs). One caught off the coast of California in 1961 weighed 858 kg (1908 lbs).

Largest tortoise
A giant tortoise of Aldabra Island in the Indian Ocean caught in 1847 weighed 405kg (900 lbs), or nearly twice the usual weight for this tortoise.

Largest snake
The anaconda of South America usually measures up to 6 m (20 ft) long. Claims of over 9 m (30 ft) are probably exaggerated. The lengths of snakes are often exaggerated.

Longest-lived tortoise
A male Marion's tortoise brought to Mauritius in 1766 was accidentally killed in 1918 at the age of over 152 years.

Tu'imalilia was the name given to a large tortoise which was said to have been presented to the King of Tonga by Captain Cook, in 1773. Tonga is an island in the South Pacific. This tortoise died on May 19, 1966. This would make it 191 years of age.

A common box turtle of the United States lived 138 years.

A European pond tortoise lived more than 120 years.

A garden tortoise died in Lambeth Palace, in London, in the 18th century. It had lived 102 or 125 years. Nobody is sure which of these two ages is correct.

Fastest swimming four-legged animal
The Pacific leatherback turtle has been timed swimming at 35 k.p.h. (22 m.p.h.).

Distance swum by estuarine crocodile
A 4.5 m (15 ft) estuarine crocodile crossed at least 960 km (600 miles) of open landless sea from the Solomon Islands to an island north of Fiji.

Speeds of reptiles

	k.p.h.	m.p.h.
Basilisk (running on hind legs)	10.80	6.80
Bearded lizard (running on hind legs)	19.30	12.00
Black mamba	16.00	10.00
California boa	0.30	0.22
Collared lizard	25.70	16.00
Coral king snake	1.20	0.72
Fringe-footed sand lizard	24.00	15.00
Gopher snake	1.85	1.18
Grass snake (on land)	8.00	5.00
Indian race-runner lizard	28.90	18.00
Leatherback turtle (swimming)	35.00	22.00
Patch-nosed snake	2.40	1.43
Red racer snake	6.40	4.00
Sidewinder	3.20	2.04
Spineless soft-shelled turtle	16.00	10.00

The most deadly of all venomous land snakes
The tiger snake of southern Australia carries enough venom to kill 118 sheep. One tiger snake had enough venom to kill 387 sheep.

The largest recorded animal to be swallowed by a snake
An impala antelope of 58 kg (130 lbs) was removed from a 4.8 m (16 ft) African rock python in 1955. The snake was not much heavier than its victim.

Snakes and the cold
In Europe the adder can live north of the Arctic Circle, at 68°N latitude. It also lives as high as 3048 m (10,000 ft) in the Swiss Alps. The most northerly snake in America is the common garter snake which is found in Labrador and the Yukon, at 67°N latitude. Another garter snake lives at 3692 m (12,000 ft) in the mountains of Mexico and the Mexican dusky rattlesnake lives at 4429 m (14,500 ft). The highest of all is the Himalayan pit-viper that may be found at 4877 m (16,000 ft) in the Himalayas.

Hibernation
When the air temperature drops below 10°C (50°F) the European adder starts searching for a place in which to rest for the winter. It comes out again in spring when the temperature reaches a little more than this.

The time spent in hibernation by snakes may be 105 days in southern Europe, 150 days in Denmark and 275 days in the extreme north.

Numbers of eggs laid by snakes
The number of eggs depends on the species and the size of the snake. The European grass snake lays 8–53, the chequered keel-back snake of southern Asia lays 8–88 eggs. An anaconda lays 4–82 eggs.

Live birth
Among snakes that give birth to living young, the puff adder may have a litter of 23–56, the common garter snake between 3 and 85.

Size of young
The egg of a European grass snake is 31 mm (about an inch) long, the young hatching from it are up to 16.5 cm (6.5 ins) long. Young anacondas are about 1 m (3.3 ft) long when first hatched.

Growth of tortoises
The warmer it is the more tortoises grow. Years ago giant tortoises brought to Europe and kept in zoos did not grow any bigger. Then, when they were kept in heated houses, at temperatures similar to those of their native home in the tropics, they increased their weight by ten times in seven years.

All about snake bites
The number of people bitten by snakes each year throughout the world is 400,000. The number that die from snake bite each year throughout the world is between 30,000 and 40,000.

The worst hit is Burma with 15 people who die out of every 100,000 of the population.

Facts and Figures

The rate is highest there because so many people go bare-foot or wear only sandals, but in India, Ceylon and Brazil, where the same is true, the death rate is between 4.1 and 5.4 per 100,000. In Australia, where 77 per cent of the snakes are venomous, there are only six deaths a year for ten million of population.

In the United States the death rate used to be 90 people a year but since anti-venines have been used it has dropped to 34. In Australia it used to be 20 people per 10,000,000, but with the use of anti-venines this has dropped to six.

Sheep and cattle are also killed by snake bite in many parts of the world. In Colorado 300 sheep out of 100,000 are bitten and 60 per cent of these die of it. On one ranch in California of 1,840 hectares (4,600 acres) the death rate for cattle from snake bite in one year was 2.2 per thousand.

When a snake bites to defend itself it is said to strike. That is, it raises its head and the front part of its body, usually in the shape of an S. Then it lunges at its enemy. It strikes faster than the eye can follow. The actual speed is, however, slower than the speed of a man's fist when he punches someone. Measurements show it is about 2.4 m (8 ft) a second.

Do baby snakes feed?
It is usually said that baby snakes eat worms and slugs. So far nobody has proved this to be true and it is still not known what baby snakes eat.

Probably they do not eat at all for the first few months.

The third eye
Nobody is sure what the tuatara uses its third eye for. Some scientists now believe that when the sun becomes too hot the third eye tells the tuatara to go into its burrow where it is cooler.

AMPHIBIANS

First amphibian
The oldest known amphibian, known as Ichthyostega, lived in Greenland over 300 million years ago.

Largest amphibian
The Chinese giant salamander averages 1 m (39.7 ins) in length and weighs up to 13 kg (28.6 lb). The largest known, caught in southern China 50 years ago, measured 1.5 m (5 ft) long.

Largest frog
A female Goliath frog caught in West Africa was 81.5 cm (32.08 ins) long with its legs extended and weighed 3.3 kg (7.5 lbs).

Largest toad
The marine toad of tropical South America. A female caught in 1965 was 23.8 cm (9.37 ins) long with its legs extended and weighed 1.3 kg (2.70 lbs).

Smallest amphibian
The arrow-poison frog of Cuba, the largest measure only 8.5–12.4 mm (0.33–0.48ins).

Longest-lived amphibian
A male Japanese giant salamander lived in the aquarium of the Amsterdam Zoo for 55 years.

Finest jumper
A male African sharp-nosed frog, known as Leaping Lena, only 5 cm (2 ins) long, covered 9.8 m (32.4 ft) in three consecutive jumps in Cape Town in 1954.

Greatest number of jumps
A spring peeper tree frog made 120 consecutive jumps in 1952 after being placed in the middle of a lawn. The spring peeper tree frog lives in the United States and is given this name because it calls *peep-peep* in spring, a welcome sign that winter is at an end.

Longest distance covered by gliding frog
The gliding frog of Malaya, Sarawak and Borneo can glide up to 30 m (100 ft) from one tree to another.

Largest number of eggs
Some frogs and toads lay more eggs than any other land vertebrate. The record is held by a Woodhouse's toad of North America which laid 25,650 eggs. A square-marked or leopard toad of Africa ran it a close second by laying over 24,000 at one sitting.

Most poisonous
The most poisonous animal in the world is the kokoi arrow-poison frog of Colombia, South America. It has been claimed that only 0.0001 g (0.0000004 ounces) of this poison is needed to kill a man.

Widest range
The common toad probably has the widest range of habitat of any living animal. It has been found as high as 7,900 m (26,200 ft) in the Himalayas and at a depth of 335 m (1115 ft) in a mine.

Calls of frogs and toads and what they resemble
Greenhouse frog (Cuba and West Indies: introduced into United States): short whistling notes like the cheeping of ducklings.
Mexican burrowing toad: a hoarse cry like that of a bird.
Cuban tree frog: snores.
Golden tree frog (Australia): like a mallet and chisel being used by a stone-mason or the distant sound of cow-bells.
Senegal striped frog: like the popping of corks.
Bamboo climbing frog (South-East Asia): coughs then crows like a rooster.
Eastern narrow-mouthed toad (United States): sounds like the bleating of sheep.

GLOSSARY

Carnivorous
Meat eating, feeding on flesh of animals, especially those with red flesh.

Cloaca
The cavity at the rear end of birds, amphibians, reptiles, most fishes and some mammals. This serves as the exit for both the faeces and urine and in females it also serves as the birth canal.

Courtship
Behaviour which occurs during the breeding season between two animals of the same species but of different sexes. After the courtship they mate and produce young.

Embryo
The name given to the baby of an animal before it is born live or hatches from an egg.

Extinct
A species which has died out is said to have become extinct.

Faeces
Waste material left after food is digested and when it is passed to the outside as dung or droppings.

Fossil
From the Latin word meaning "to be dug up". Fossils are the remains of plants and animals of the past which are found embedded in rocks or buried in the earth.

Freshwater
Water which is not salty, for example the water in ponds and streams.

Gills
The breathing organs of water-living animals, into which impure blood flows to be oxygenated (purified) by oxygen from the surrounding water.

Gullet
The tube through which food passes from the mouth to the stomach.

Herbivorous
Plant eating, as opposed to meat eating.

Hibernation
The inactive, or restful state of some animals during the winter in cold countries. Also called winter sleep.

Infertile
This term is applied to an animal which is not able to produce babies or to eggs that will not hatch.

Ligament
Tough, flexible tissue which connects muscles to bones or sometimes binds two bones together.

Lungs
The breathing organs of animals which take their oxygen from the air.

Parasite
An animal or plant that feeds at the expense of another animal or plant.

Proboscis
A tubular nose or a tube coming from the mouth which is used for sucking.

Scales
Small, thin membranes or horny modifications of the skin in many fishes and reptiles. These usually overlap and form a complete covering for the body.

Sloughing
The term applied to the way in which snakes and lizards cast off the outer skin from time to time.

Sperm
Male cells which fertilize the female's eggs to produce offspring. Sperm is short for spermatazoa.

Tentacle
A thin, hair-like or finger-like organ in animals, which is used to feel with.

Territory
A piece of ground which an animal takes as its own. For animals which live in water, a territory may be made up of a volume of water. Although the territory is not marked out, most animals know when they are not in their own territory. If an animal goes into another animal's territory, the owner will try to drive it out.

Tropical
The part of the earth that lies between the Tropic of Cancer and the Tropic of Capricorn. This is the warmest part of the earth.

Vertebrate
An animal with a backbone.

Vocal sac
A bag of skin in the throat or in the side of the mouth used by an animal to make its voice sound louder.

THE ANIMAL KINGDOM

The Animal Kingdom is divided into a number of phyla (singular = phylum). Each phylum is divided into several classes, each class into orders, each order into families, each family containing one or more genera (singular = genus), each genus containing one or more species. Thus, the garden tortoise (*Testudo hermanni*) belongs to the phylum Chordata, of which the Vertebrata is a subphylum. Within the Chordata it is placed in the class Reptilia, order Testudines, family Testudinidae, genus *Testudo*, species *hermanni*.

CLASSIFICATION

CLASS Amphibia
  Order Gymnophiona (Caecilians 4 families)
  Order Caudata (or Urodela) (Newts and salamanders 8 families)
  Order Anura (or Salientia) (Frogs and toads 16 or 15 families)

CLASS Reptilia
  Order Rhynchocephalia (Tuatara 1 family)
  Order Testudines, (Turtles, tortoises, terrapins 12 families)
  Order Crocodilia (Crocodiles, alligators, caimans, gavials 3 families)
  Order Squamata
    Sub Order Sauria (Lizards)
    Family Gekkonidae (Geckos)
    Family Iguanidae (Iguanas)
    Family Chamaeleontidae (Chameleons)
    Family Lacertidae (True Lizards)
    Family Agamidae (Agamas)
    Family Scincidae (Skinks)
    Family Varanidae (Monitors)
    Family Dibamidae (Burrowing Lizards)
    Family Teiidae (Teiids)
    Family Xantusiidae (Night Lizards)
    Family Pygopodidae (Pygopodids)
    Family Cordylidae (Plated Lizards)
    Family Anguidae (Anguids)
    Family Helodermatidae (Poisonous Lizards)
    Family Lanthanotidae (Bornean Earless Monitor)
    Family Amphisbaenidae (Worm Lizards)
    Family Trogonophidae (Worm Lizards)
    Family Xenosauridae (Crocodile Lizards)
    Family Anniellidae (Shovel Snouted Legless Lizards)
    Sub Order Serpentes (Snakes 12 families)

How to Draw

A frog

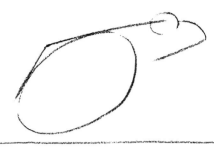

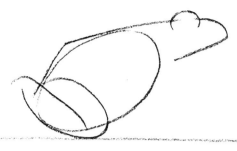

1. Draw an egg shape for the body which is tipped up at the front.

2. Add neck, head shape with eye and small "hump" on the back.

3. Start back legs, with the "knee" resting on the ground.

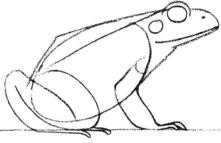

4. Complete back legs to the toes and add front legs.

5. Add toes to front and back legs, indicating features such as eye and mouth.

6. Complete drawing by inking in and joining lines smoothly.

A snake

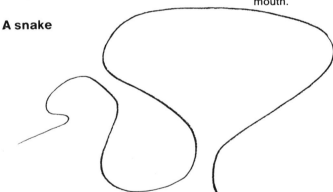

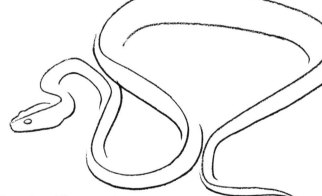

I. This curvy shape will be the snake's backbone.

2. Fill in shape by adding parts that rest on the ground.

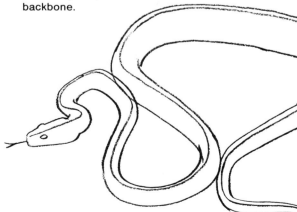

3. Now add lines for the other side of body.

4. Complete by inking in and decorate with patterns on each side of the backbone.

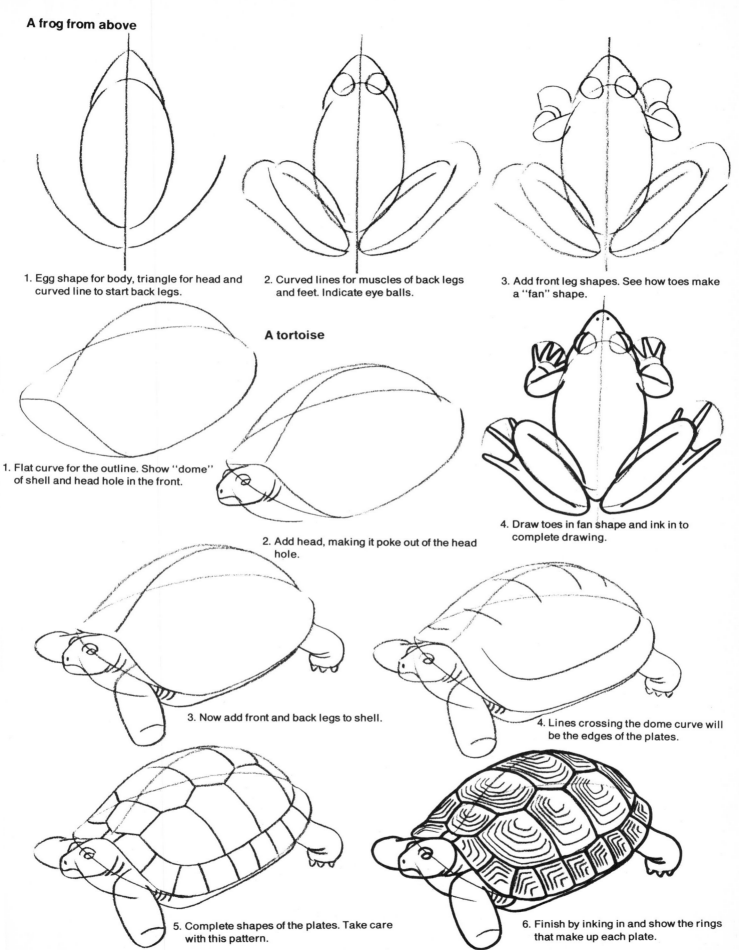

A frog from above

1. Egg shape for body, triangle for head and curved line to start back legs.

2. Curved lines for muscles of back legs and feet. Indicate eye balls.

3. Add front leg shapes. See how toes make a "fan" shape.

4. Draw toes in fan shape and ink in to complete drawing.

A tortoise

1. Flat curve for the outline. Show "dome" of shell and head hole in the front.

2. Add head, making it poke out of the head hole.

3. Now add front and back legs to shell.

4. Lines crossing the dome curve will be the edges of the plates.

5. Complete shapes of the plates. Take care with this pattern.

6. Finish by inking in and show the rings that make up each plate.

53

Keeping a Vivarium

How to make a pond

Dig a hole in the ground 20 cms deep and 20 cms square. Get a piece of waterproof sheeting, such as polythene. You would need a piece

75 cms × 75 cms for a pond this size. Line the pond with the polythene, keeping it in place with stones on the edge of it.

What to keep in a vivarium

A vivarium is a container or area of ground to keep animals that do not live in water. Most reptiles are suitable for keeping in a vivarium. Lizards are the best reptiles to keep as pets in a vivarium. It is also possible to keep toads, frogs and newts in a vivarium, but they should be allowed to go free in the spring, so that they can go to another pond to breed.

An outdoor vivarium

An outdoor vivarium need not be very big as long as it has the things that the animals need in it. It can be about one metre square. The vivarium should have sun and shade. Although the animals may like to bask in the sun for quite a long time, they should have somewhere to shade themselves if they want to. Rocks or big stones are the best way of making shelter. The animals can then hide among or under the rocks where it should be very cool.

The atmosphere in the vivarium should be as damp as possible. If you dig a small pond (the diagram below shows you a quick and easy way of doing this) and keep it well filled with water the air will stay damp.

The animals will probably not go into the water at all, but their skin would become much too dry if the air around them was very dry. Make sure that the water is clean. You should not have to change it as often out of doors as you would change it in an indoor vivarium.

If possible it is a good idea to use a wall as one side of your vivarium, and wire netting for the other three sides. Bend the netting over at the top into the vivarium so that the animals cannot escape. The netting should have very small holes in it for the same reason.

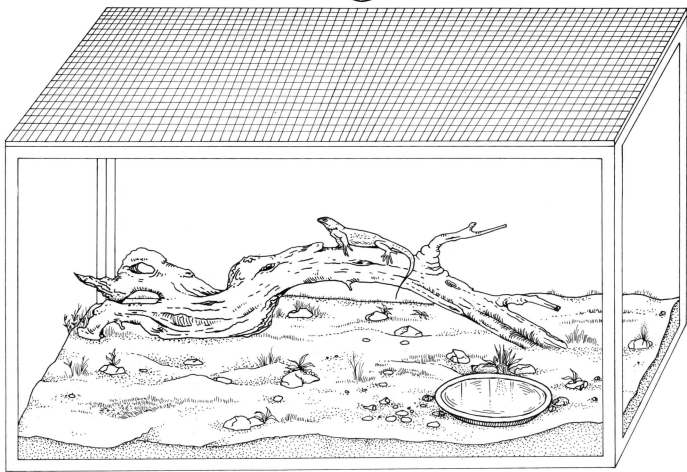

An indoor vivarium

You can keep the same animals in an indoor vivarium as in an outdoor one. The vivarium can be made in a glass tank with straight sides.

Like the outdoor vivarium, you should put a bowl of water, some large stones, gravel and moss, and perhaps a small branch into the vivarium. A bulb hanging over the tank replaces the sun. It is important that the vivarium is kept clean.

Food

You must feed the animals in both the outdoor and the indoor vivarium.

You can buy meal worms from a pet shop as the main food for all the animals. They also like gentles, which you can buy from a fish-tackle shop.

It is best to give the animals fresh food every day and to remove old food.

Hibernation

In October the animals will want to rest for the winter. Lizards, toads and newts need a dry place for the winter, but frogs like somewhere damp. If you dig a hole, put a box into it and fill the box with moss, dry leaves and straw, the lizards, toads and newts will crawl into it when the weather gets cold. Make sure that the box will not get filled with water if it rains. As frogs need a damp spot to rest in, they may rest in the pond if there are plants growing in it. The animals may come out on a warm, sunny day. Put some food out for them in case they are hungry.

Overcrowding and mixing

It is very important that your animals should have enough space to live in. If you are not sure how big your vivarium should be, ask at your petshop. It is not a good idea to put different animals together unless you are sure that they will not, for example, eat each other. Ask at your petshop about this as well.

Keeping Terrapins

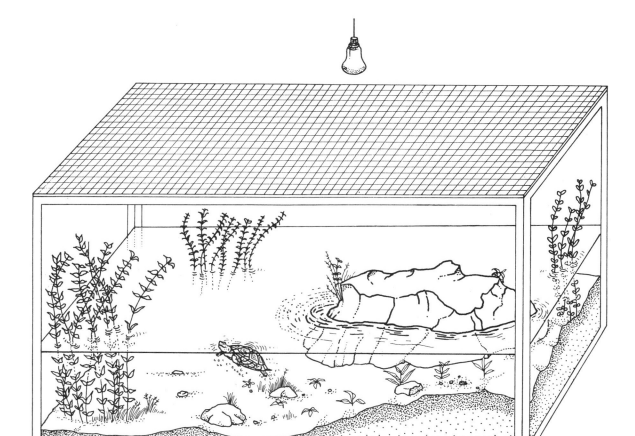

An aquavivarium

Terrapins can be kept in a tank, pond or an aquavivarium. An aquavivarium is a vivarium with some water in it. Terrapins swim a great deal, but they also like to rest on rocks out of the water. The aquavivarium should have gravel or stones on the bottom with a rock that is partly out of the water. Terrapins do not need plants for food, but these can be kept for decoration.

When it is warm an aquavivarium can be kept outside. When the weather is colder you must keep it indoors with an electric bulb over it to keep the terrapins warm.

Food

Terrapins eat meat. You can give them small amounts of tinned cat or dog food, raw fish or raw meat, or earthworms. It is best to put a fairly small amount of food in the water about two or three times a week. You will soon see how much the terrapins want each week. Tinned dog or cat food is good for terrapins because it has extra vitamins in it.

Cleaning

It is very important that the water is kept clean. When you change the water make sure that the new water is the same temperature as the water you are replacing.

Soft shells

Some terrapins have soft shells. This means that there is too little chalk (calcium) in the water. You can sprinkle powdered cuttlebone, which you can buy in petshops, on the water to add calcium. Better still, give them pond snails to eat. The snails' shells will supply the calcium.

The terrapins that are sold in petshops are usually babies. They are very small and very attractive, but they may not live for more than a year. However, if you look after your terrapins properly, they should survive the first year. If they do they should live for many more years.

Keeping Tadpoles

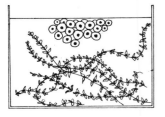

Feeding the tadpoles

If you want to keep tadpoles, collect some frogspawn from a pond in spring. Put the spawn into a tank filled with water and plants from the pond. When the tadpoles hatch they will start to eat the pond weed. Soon they become more active and will want to eat meat. You can hang a piece of meat in the water by a thread of cotton.

If the water in the tank is dirty it is best to renew it with water from the pond. If this is not possible use rain water or water from the tap that has been standing for a few days.

From tadpoles to froglets

It is important to notice when the tadpoles are turning into froglets. When the tadpoles have four legs you should transfer them to a shallow dish with a rock sticking out of the water. Then they can sit on the rock and breathe in air.

Froglets usually leave their pond when they have still got a small tail. It is best to take your froglets back to their pond when they have reached this stage as it is difficult to feed them.

Sometimes a garden tortoise will lay an egg on top of the ground. This egg will be infertile and will never hatch. If you find some eggs buried in your garden or see your tortoise dig a pit in which to lay her eggs, these may hatch. Put the eggs into a box filled with sand and earth. The box should be kept in a warm cupboard or underneath a light bulb. The sand should be kept at about 20°C. Test it with a thermometer. The eggs must always be kept in the same position as they were laid in. Do not turn them over and over to examine them.

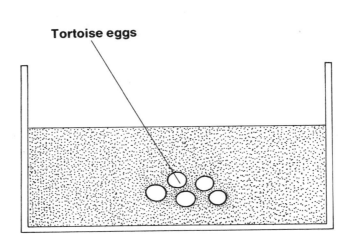

Tortoise eggs

Keeping Tortoises

Tortoises are not dull

Some people think that tortoises are slow and dull animals. They can be interesting pets but they do need to be properly cared for.

When you buy a tortoise there are three signs you ought to look for. Its eyes should be bright, not watering; it should be heavy compared with other tortoises in the shop; and it should draw its head and legs into its shell as soon as you pick it up.

Where to keep your tortoise

Although a tortoise can be kept on a balcony, it is best kept in a garden. The tortoise should be kept in a pen, as it may wander away if it is not fenced in.

A wire netting fence of about half a metre high should be dug firmly into the ground, otherwise the tortoise may dig underneath it.

House and food

The tortoise should have shelter for the night. A wooden box or a cardboard box makes a very good shelter. The box should be lined with straw, which you must change very often. Outside the box you must keep a shallow dish of water for the tortoise to drink from. In hot weather a tortoise likes to wallow in water. So the dish should be large enough for it to sit comfortably in it, and shallow enough for it to climb in and out easily.

Tortoises will eat almost any green plants. Make sure that they do not eat plants in your garden.

You should give your tortoise fresh food like lettuce or dandelion leaves each day. It will not always eat the same amount every day, but it should not come to any harm if it does not eat for several days—tortoises can live for at least a fortnight without food if they do not want to eat.

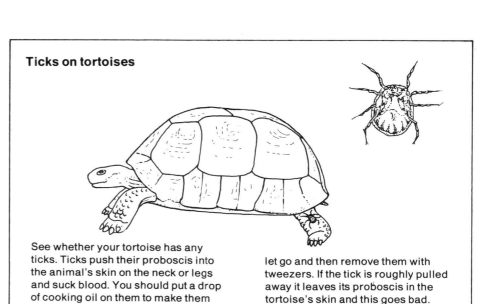

Ticks on tortoises

See whether your tortoise has any ticks. Ticks push their proboscis into the animal's skin on the neck or legs and suck blood. You should put a drop of cooking oil on them to make them let go and then remove them with tweezers. If the tick is roughly pulled away it leaves its proboscis in the tortoise's skin and this goes bad.

Hibernation

In Autumn the tortoise's movements become slow and it will show signs of looking for somewhere to go to sleep through the winter. Small tortoises should not be allowed to hibernate but must be brought indoors and kept in a warm room. A well-grown tortoise should be put in a box, not less than half a metre square, preferably much larger, filled with torn up and crumpled newspaper, hay, straw or dried leaves, with a lid with holes in it for ventilation. The lid should not be nailed or tied down. Once the tortoise has gone to sleep it should not be disturbed, although it does not hurt to lift the lid gently to see how it is getting on. The box should not be brought indoors but kept in an unheated outhouse or in a cellar, one that is free of rats. In the spring the tortoise will wake when warm weather is here. When it starts to move on a warm sunny day give it a warm bath, just the lower part of the shell and the legs, and bathe round the mouth.

A tortoise will lose weight during hibernation and you may like to weigh your pet at different times of the year to see what progress it is making. If you keep a record of the weights this will be quite instructive. A tortoise weighing about 2.70 kg (6 lbs) may lose nearly 0.22 kg ($\frac{1}{2}$ lb) in weight while it is hibernating.

Don'ts

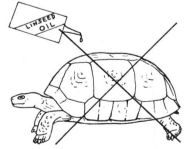

Don't polish the shell of your tortoise with either wax or linseed oil, because it stops up the pores in the shell. If you feel you must polish the shell use olive oil because it is harmless.

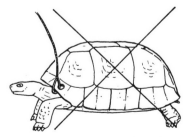

Don't try to tether your tortoise by boring a hole through the edge of its shell so that you can tie a piece of string through it. The string may strangle the tortoise. Also the tortoise may snap off the corner of its shell trying to escape.

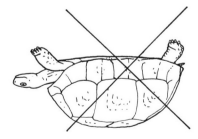

Don't let your tortoise lie on its back. If your tortoise climbs among rocks it may fall on to its back. If the ground is uneven it may be able to right itself.

Index to Pictures and Text

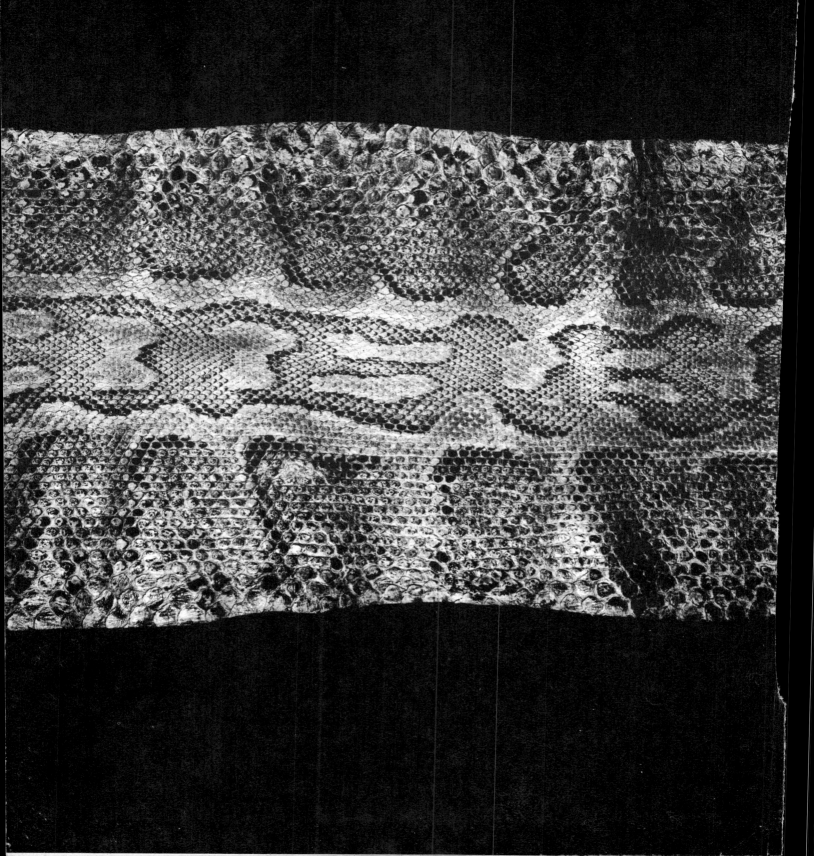